THE BOOK ON WOW

How to Blow Away Your Clients and Everyone Else in Your Life!

ASH WALANI
and
RAYMOND AARON

First edition published by 10-10-10 Publishing

www.BookonWOW.com
www.awcreativemedia.com

Copyright © 2018 Ash Walani and Raymond Aaron

ISBN: 978-1-77277-199-2

Ash Walani has asserted his right under the Copyright, Designs, and Patents Act, 1988 to be identified as the author of this work.

All rights reserved. No portion of this book may be reproduced mechanically, electronically, or by any other means, including photocopying, without permission of the publisher or author except in the case of brief quotations embodied in critical articles and reviews. It is illegal to copy this book, post it to a website, or distribute it by any other means without permission from the publisher or author.

Limits of Liability and Disclaimer of Warranty

The author and publisher shall not be liable for your misuse of the enclosed material. This book is strictly for informational and educational purposes.

Warning – Disclaimer

The purpose of this book is to educate and entertain. The author and/or publisher do not guarantee that anyone following these techniques, suggestions, tips, ideas, or strategies will become successful. The author and/or publisher shall have neither liability nor responsibility to anyone with respect to any loss or damage caused, or alleged to be caused, directly or indirectly by the information contained in this book.

Publisher 10-10-10 Publishing Markham, ON Canada

Printed in Canada and the United States

Dedication

To the WOWs of my world, Anyssa and Armaan,
you're the reason I create anything.

To Shazia, truly, love personified
and the best WOW of my life.

And to KM, my mentor, "The Boss",
a guide and all around inspiring human.

Dedication

Contents

Acknowledgements ix

Foreword xi

SECTION 1:
Applying WOW to Your Personal Life 1

CHAPTER 1:
Those First Moments of WOW 3
    A Teacher's Praise 5
    Living a Life of unWOW 7
    Important WOW Concepts 13
    How to Get The Most Out of This Book 16

CHAPTER 2:
How to Completely Overwhelm
Your Spouse With WOW 19
    Starting Over 21
    How to WOW Your Spouse 25
    What Do You Want Most? 31

CHAPTER 3:
How to Develop WOW With Your Kids 33
    Qualities Kids With WOW Possess 34
    5 Ways to Develop WOW in Your Kids 36
    The Results of Raising WOW Kids 40

CHAPTER 4:
How to Keep Your Friends & Family Close With The Power of WOW 43
    WOWing Others Means WOWing Yourself First 46
    The Catalyst That Changed My Life 47
    WOWing Your Parents 48
    What About the In-Laws 52
    How to Have WOW Relationships With Your Siblings 53
    WOWing Your Friends 55

SECTION 2:
Applying WOW to Your Professional Life 57

CHAPTER 5:
How to WOW Your Employer Into Raises And Promotions 59
    38 Ways to WOW Your Boss 61

CHAPTER 6:
How to WOW Your Clients to Brand Advocacy 75
    What is Branding? 76
    Personal Branding 77

Contents

The Branding Ladder 77
How to WOW Your Customers Up
The Branding Ladder 83
Business Card 83
Communication Skills 84
Keep Your Promises 85
5 Simple Ways to WOW Your Clients 85
It's Time to Start 87

CHAPTER 7:
How to Create a Team of WOW
With Your Staff/Co-Workers 89

How to Create A WOW Team 90
How to Keep The WOW Going With
Your Existing Staff/Co-workers? 95
What Are The Results of a WOW Team 96

CHAPTER 8:
The Directors of WOW and unWOW 97

The Director of WOW 99
Create a Culture of WOW 100
The Director of unWOW 101

CHAPTER 9:
Springing Into Action 105

The Starting Place For Personal WOW 108
The Starting Place For Professional WOW 110
We're Finally Here 113

Acknowledgements

My journey into writing would not have been possible without the support of my loving wife and amazing children. Thank you for always being an inspiration and with all of my pursuits, standing by me no matter how crazy they sound. Shazia, waking up to you every morning, is still the only fuel I need.

To my amazing mother, Shirin, you have stood by me, always allowing me to follow my dreams. The untold sacrifices you have made for your children remain saint worthy.

To my late father, Amin, thank you for helping me learn the powerful road to forgiveness and in giving one's heart, wholly.

Thank you, Raymond Aaron, for being the star that lit the way to authorship.

To his brilliant wife and my friend Karyn, essentially a human wish provider and dream maker. I am humbled by your generosity and your gifting's. Thank you for listening, offering me advice, and supporting me through everything.

To Mr. Launder and Ms. Small, wherever you are, who knew I'd be writing this book someday. Teachers like you are gifts that the world is way too short of these days.

To all my colleagues, staff and compadres at Staxi! I love you guys so much. Lori, my beautiful Potts!! Helen, Mi'lady and my UK bestie!! Shout out to Dawnie Marie!

To the ever loyal Bhav and Brooks, for simple and real, unconditional friendship. I love you both.

Thank you Kim Thompson-Pinder for being my editor who helped to make this book shine.

To all and everyone in my life, for their encouragement and advice when needed and even when not. Thank you for helping me keep things in perspective.

And God knows, that I know, that He knows that He's got my back . . . always.

Foreword

THE BEST WORD to describe this book is WOW. Ash Walani and Raymond Aaron have really captured what it means to live a life of Wondrous Outstanding Worth.

The Book on WOW!: How to Blow Away Your Clients and Everyone Else in Your Life will help you create WOW in all the areas of your life, starting with yourself, then expanding out to your spouse, kids, family, and friends. In each area they give you sound teaching and practical ideas that you can start using NOW.

Relationships with family and friends may often keep you under constant stress and pull you away from your dreams and goals instead of supporting you towards them. What can you do? You can learn to live a life of WOW by following the tools that Ash and Raymond teach you in this book.

You may be struggling financially, not even making it from paycheck to paycheck, hoping for something better but not knowing how to get there. Ash and Raymond reveal strategies to use in your professional life and shows you how to use WOW to get raises, earn promotions, brand yourself for success, create a WOW team and so much more.

Mentally and emotionally you may be a mess and haven't learned how to master your thoughts and feelings to create success. From communication skills, to keeping your promise, this book will help you to WOW your clients, build a great career for yourself, and improve your mental wellbeing.

If you follow the teachings in this book, you will find your life going from blah to amazing, as you see WOW working in your life. I highly recommend this book as a must-read as you learn that there is more to life and the path to get there!!!

Loral Langemeier
The Millionaire Maker

SECTION 1

Applying WOW to Your Personal Life

CHAPTER 1

Those First Moments of WOW

Ash's First Insight Into Wow

> *"A true artist is not one who is inspired,*
> *but one who inspires others."*
> —Salvador Dali

THERE ARE MOMENTS in your life which at the time seemed ordinary, yet as you look back on them, you realize that they had a profound effect on the course of your life. I have had a few such moments.

One of them occurred when I was 21-years-old. I had decided to open a clothing store in Toronto, and even though I didn't know a lot about customer service, I soon learned a valuable lesson in WOWing your clients. Most of my suppliers had showrooms in Montreal, so I would often travel there to see what was new and coming out soon.

When I was in Montreal, I felt like a king! As I entered a supplier's showroom, they would offer me my favourite drink, a chilled Perrier water. The Perrier was always chilled to the right temperature, plus they never forgot the lemon wedge! They knew my taste in music and had the specific songs that I liked playing in the background. You were wined and dined and had a personal session where even the sales rep would model the clothing for you. Everything was glamourous.

They WOWed me so much, that I felt indebted to the point where even if the clothing line were average, I would be so caught up in wanting to buy from them, that sometimes I wouldn't even look at the price point. If I had been more seasoned in business, I would have been more careful about that because my business partner and I ended up having to close the business.

Nevertheless . . .

I learned a valuable lesson in the power of WOW when dealing with my customers. It made me realize that a customer was something very important. Those suppliers had gone the extra mile with me and it had made an impression, so I learned early on to do the same.

We would have clients' clothes picked out in their favourite colours before the client arrived. Dress shirts would be opened and hung on hangers, so trying them on became easy and efficient. I, too, made sure their favorite music was playing, or if they loved *café au lait*, it was there and prepared the exact way they enjoyed it.

If I knew it was their wife I had to impress, I would make it a point to recall her children's names or what we spoke about the last time they were in. Sometimes I would make notes, and sometimes I would just remember. My business partner was especially good at this, and even though he was notoriously abrasive and snooty with our clients in an almost comical way, they loved him for his distinctive touch.

Anything we could do to make the customer feel appreciated, we did it. The way we dealt with our customers made them very loyal to us. They knew that they could count on us to go over and above what was expected.

So, that's how I translated what I had learned from those suppliers to my customers, and it was the difference between them buying maybe one shirt or turning that sale into an entire seasonal wardrobe. (Not to mention that it created some awesome repeat customers--an always-welcome bonus!)

A Teacher's Praise

Everyone thought I was in love with my Grade 7 teacher. At the time, if you had asked me I would have said 'no,' but as I think back on it, I probably did have a crush on her. Yes, I was a 12-year-old pubescent teen with raging hormones, easily distracted by a beautiful older woman, but more than that, her positive encouragement had an enormous impact on my life. I still admire her in my heart to this day.

I started writing in Grade 7 with my first small novel, and when I showed it to my teacher, she was so impressed with it that she sent me to a writer's conference. It was an amazing experience for a 12-year-old.

Everything about the conference WOWed me. The conference was held in a beautiful hotel in a gorgeous rural setting that inspired the mind. It was a place full of life. I was a suburban kid from very humble beginnings and to be able to learn from other authors was truly uplifting. Not only did it validate my dream that writing was worth pursuing but planted seeds that are now coming to life at this point in my life. This book is proof of that.

Even with that experience, I never considered myself a writer. Recently, however, I edited my first screenplay that I had first started about six years ago. At the time when I wrote it, my wife and I were separated for nine months while she was studying abroad. (I will share more about how the power of WOW saved our marriage in Chapter 2.)

Although it only took me three months to initially complete, it sat in my briefcase for a year. I never shared it with anyone. When I finally did show it to someone, I wasn't thrilled with what they said. So, I hid it away again. Finally, this year I gathered up my courage, and I hired another writer and said, "Here's my screenplay. It's 157 pages. I know it's too much. Can you go through it and make it better?" And he did.

The first time he read it, he emailed me and said, "I know you say you don't call yourself a writer, but you're wrong. I teach writing, and I read screenplays for a living. Your work needs polish, and of course, it's not perfect, but it is better than 90 percent of the ones I read from my students."

I was shocked. I had considered myself a graphic artist, specializing in visual and abstract styles, yes, but not a writer. When I looked at the screenplay, he didn't rewrite much. He essentially cut out the stuff that wasn't important and made it look more professional.

So, what my seventh-grade teacher said was true, and after blocking it for 30 years, I now know that I am a writer. My life has changed because of that WOW seed that was planted within me all those years ago.

Here is a key point: you never know what kind of effect those little moments might have on others. Every WOW will bear fruit in one way or another, so take every opportunity to demonstrate WOW in all areas of your life.

Living a Life of unWOW

So many people live a life of unWOW and don't even realize how much more there is. They live lives of quiet desperation and unhappiness. They think, "That is what life is supposed to be like." It is sad, and by recognizing areas of unWOW, it is my hope that you will set yourself free and become a person who lives a life of WOW! Let's look at the biggest reasons people find themselves living a life of unWOW.

1. The Blame Game

Everything bad that happens is everybody else's fault. "She cheated on me." "He did this." "She never loved me." "It's my boss' fault I never got that raise." "My parents never gave me any opportunities." "The teacher didn't like me-- that is why I got bad grades." "I was late because of traffic" and so on.

I have a close friend who acts that way constantly. I warned her that if she continues down that path, she is going to live her entire life in perpetual bitterness and unhappiness. The entire course of her life will be a series of unWOWs.

The way to get out of the blame game is to learn the difference between responsibility and blame. Being responsible doesn't necessarily mean you're to blame for it, but accepting the fact that everything in your life is showing up because you either created it or allowed it to happen, is a hard pill to swallow. It is easier to find fault than to take the harder steps to making things better.

When you can accept responsibility –truly take the reins and say you are not the victim, then you can begin to live a life of WOW. The amazing thing about taking responsibility is that, once you do, you are in control of your life. You can become the person you want to be and achieve the results that others think are impossible.

2. Freedom of Truth

If you're going to have a WOW relationship, you need to understand this concept. Especially in relationships like a marriage where it can go to hell after two, five, seven, ten years or more.

We don't always tell the truth to each other as partners, as lovers, as friends or even as siblings and parents. In most cases, we spend our entire lives behind masks. We create these masks to be seen as likable characters. We accept, we hide, we lie. We do things because we just don't want to rock the boat.

Those First Moments of WOW

We will tell someone we love that they look great in an outfit (when they don't) because we don't want to hurt their feelings. We call them little white lies and we say they are harmless. We say it is to protect others. In the end, these lies deteriorate us on the inside, whether we like to accept that or not. Carrying the burden of the untruths takes a heavy toll. If we knowingly tell untruths, the entire world becomes a place we cannot trust. This inadvertently leads us to attempting to protect others from ourselves. It keeps us hidden.

When my wife and I were reconciling, we went through a coached process where we were completely honest with each other about everything. It's not an easy thing to do. It got ugly, trust me. Immediately after a particularly bad session, I was so angry that I was ready to blow up my wife, the coach and pretty much the world! In that moment, I saw how anger could get away from you, and the term, "crime of passion" made total and complete sense.

Thankfully, I saw the rage for what it was and quickly got it under control. The thing I could not understand about it was why my wife felt great immediately after the truth process. I didn't! I couldn't grasp why she seemed uplifted, and I wasn't. Then, the brilliant coach shared this insight. He told me, "It's because you haven't told the complete truth and you're still lying. She has released everything. That's why she feels happy and loving you. You can't accept it because you're upset. You're still lying about something."

That truth sucker-punched me in the stomach, to the point where my breath left me for a moment. I had to go back to the process and soul search and revisit the truth

I was not willing to share. Once I could get it out and share it, that invisible weight and rage disappeared. I didn't realize the weight of the burden I was carrying until it was gone. I could now also trust that she was telling the full truth.

So, the freedom of truth comes when you're able to be honest without hurting the other person. For example, my wife and I went kitchen cabinet shopping, a potentially volatile task for any couple. In <u>The Huffington Post July 31, 2013</u>, they talk about a survey that found that 12% of couples considered separation or divorce after doing major renovations. That tells you just how stressful on a marriage it can be.

In the past, I wouldn't have said anything at the time of selection then spend the rest of the next 10 to 15 years hating those cabinets and her every time I looked at them. That acidic bitterness just reeks unWOW and even worst, that one decision can affect your marriage for over ten years!

Now, with our new paradigm of honesty, I simply tell her my truth, without attacking her verbally. In the case of cabinets, we then worked together to find ones we both liked. It allowed me to truly spend the time with her and I listened with an open heart. Now we both appreciate them when we use them, but the process of picking them out strengthened our relationship.

I must admit; I wish I had learned the freedom of truth years ago in business. My business partner had been my best friend since grade two, but I was afraid to tell him that I was unhappy doing what we were doing. This was not about him. Remember, he was not at fault. I spent all my time keeping my feelings unexpressed, doing things I didn't want to do, or things I didn't agree with. I could not muster the courage to take charge of my life and do the things I wanted in a career. Instead, the mistakes we made compounded and probably caused us to struggle and keep the business open two years longer than necessary, causing even more financial loss in the end.

3. The Martyr Syndrome

I have seen many people who have suffered from this affliction. I have been guilty of it myself from time to time. It is a habit that leaves your life completely imbalanced, because you always put everyone else's needs above your own. But then you resent everyone else, either for taking advantage of you or never feeling acknowledged. Again, I wish to stress, that this is a life of your creation. To give or do something good should never be undertaken with the intention of having it acknowledged or being given something in return.

There are so many people who say that they are selfless, but it is an untruth. The reason I say this? Over time, they become angry and bitter. They get tired of thinking that people are always asking something of them all the time. They come to resent everyone who needs them. They create the situation, then hate the results.

True balance in life comes when you take care of your needs and can help others as well. That means from time to time that you need to say no to people because at that moment your need is more important.

Time and time again I see people who give much time to charity, which is very commendable but not if it is to the detriment of themselves or their family. Their lives remain in tatters and ruin. They help the homeless guy they see downtown and then don't have money to take care of their own family or worst their family relationships are failing.

I am not saying to avoid acts of kindness, but to truly consider the consequences of that action before doing it. Think of it like the safety rules on a plane. Put your oxygen mask on first, even before you help your child put on theirs, so you can be a real help! It applies in life as well when we are out to create WOWs!

Another type of martyr syndrome is the "Immigrant Parent Sacrifice" theory. It is where immigrant parents sacrifice everything for their kids. It doesn't matter whether you talk to Indian, Italian or Ukrainian parents. Everything is about the kids. The parents work their fingers to the bone, until they put their kids through school, give them what they want and then make a way for their future.

They never look for any kind of reciprocation, but they always hope that their kids will love and protect them because of it. The problem with that, is it comes down to martyrdom again and when the kids don't reciprocate in terms of loving them for it, they feel betrayed.

The reality is that they created an entitlement culture for their kids where everything is all about them, not the family as a whole. They did not give their children an opportunity for exchange. Meaning that many times, and even myself included, will give and give and give to our kids without asking for anything in return.

It's not about getting money back, it's about getting anything they perceive as valuable in exchange. It could be love, it could be kisses, it could be a hug, it could be anything they want, but something that the child will feel, from an early age, is giving something back. So, help me do the dishes, do some chores. It could be any kind of reciprocal kind of agreement, teaching the kids to be responsible for their part of being a WOW family.

If you don't, some bad consequences can happen. I've seen instances where the kids end up having no relationship with their parents and their parents have spent like $200,000 on their education, and they never hear from them again.

Creating a WOW family means you WOWing your kids, WHILE teaching them to take responsibility for WOWing you and others at the same time. But we will cover more about this in Chapter 3.

Important WOW Concepts

Now that we have covered what unWOW looks like, I want to go over some concepts that will be carried throughout the book as we look at all the various parts of your life and creating WOW in them.

The first concept is creating affinity, especially in business. This is where you treat people with such WOW and respect that they become your brand ambassadors. They are not only brand loyal to the point they will only buy from you, but they also tell others, without you asking them to buy from you as well.

The amazing thing about affinity is that there is mutual respect. The customer is not always right, but as you listen, as you are patient and as you are empathetic and understand why they feel that way, you can solve the issue to both of your satisfactions.

Sometimes the best affinity is also knowing when to let go. Sometimes there are customers that are not healthy and to keep affinity with the rest of your customers you need to let those go.

The next concept is Interchange of Prosperousness. It is the concept of WOWing people/customers/employees/family. It is where you go beyond what is expected.

You give them what you promised, and then, of course, you give them more. You up the quality of the material without the customer asking, or you give them those extra proofs, or you give them 10 or 15 extra units and say, even though you paid for a 100, I gave you 115. Thanks for your business. You can do this because your unit cost is lower so you've made money on the transaction and they have gotten a better deal than they expected.

It doesn't always have to be something that costs money, in fact in business, you can go bankrupt if you do that every time. But, there are almost always times where you've made extra units or your cost-per-unit is minimal so the WOW does not cost anything. Or, you can do something that only requires a bit of extra time (with no cost).

You can research their favorite music that you asked about in your past meetings and then send them a link to a new song that you think they would love or an article on a writer that they may find intriguing. There is no cost to wow them and create affinity in this way.

Also, let's say you offer a graphic design service with printing. The customer sent you a version of their logo which was inferior in quality. You could contact them and charge them an extra fee for fixing it, or you can take those few minutes, fix it for them at no charge and WOW them. Completing the job early would be a WOW, as would keeping your business open a bit later until they can get there to pick up the order.

Now let's talk about the interchange part of this. It is not just about you continually giving; there are times that you can expect things back. So, in the example above, you may ask for compensation if they choose to use the logo for something other than the purpose you created it for.

When you WOW them, they know internally and emotionally that they can trust you. That you have their best interest at heart. They feel like they want to give something back, and will work with you even if your costs may be higher than the competition because you have earned that privilege.

The Interchange of Prosperousness also applies in relationships. When you take the opportunities to WOW your spouse and they you, it creates an intimacy that nothing can ever break. I can personally tell you how special I felt when my wife did something out of the ordinary for me just because she loves me. There may be a book from my favourite author sitting on my desk when I get home or a new painting on the wall from one of my favourite artists. Then there was the time she made a secret sexual fantasy I had shared with her come alive. All these things told me in no uncertain terms that I am cherished and treasured.

There is nothing that I won't do for my wife. She is the love of my life, and after almost 30 years together I can tell you that I love her more and more each day. I couldn't imagine my life without her.

How to Get The Most Out of This Book

I encourage you to read this book from front to back and then take the one chapter that catches your heart the most and work on learning to create a meaningful WOW in that area. Once you have conquered that, it is time to move on to the next one.

Here is one thing about creating WOWs in other's lives. Each WOW act is a seed that not only bears fruit in the life of the person who receives it, but also in the person that gives it. Over time, not only will you be giving so much WOW that it will become a natural part of your life, but you will be receiving it as well.

How can you tell if something is a WOW, consider this acronym:

W – Wondrous

O – Outstanding

W – Worth

Does it create wonder and awe in the person receiving it? Then it is a WOW. Is it above average, outstanding and more than what the person is expecting? Then it is a WOW. Does it provide worth? If it does, then it is a WOW.

I encourage you to join me on this journey into Wondrous Outstanding Worth, not only in your life but in others as well. In the next chapter, we will start with the most important relationship in your life, your spouse. You will be surprised at how close I came to losing it all and how thankful I am that I didn't.

CHAPTER 2

How to Completely Overwhelm Your Spouse With WOW

Ash's Experience

"The more I think about it, the more I realize there is nothing more artistic than to love others."

—Vincent Van Gogh

I WAS ON THE brink of ending my marriage after 28 years. On the surface, everything was perfect. We were a beautiful couple and we had amazing children. The children were doing great, and we were both successful. We had everything that everybody would want in a marriage and a relationship.

From the outside, it looked good, but it was only a show. Even our kids didn't know what was going on because we hid it so well. Our kids didn't realize how much we had grown apart.

Things weren't good in our marriage, there was no connection or affinity whatsoever. I no longer knew this woman I had been married to for so long because we led very separate lives. While we were incredibly miserable, we still maintained an iota of respect and love. Truly we never wanted to hurt each other, yet we were both so angry on the inside while trying to show nothing on the outside. Of course, at some point, physically, there was nothing left.

When things aren't good in your marriage, that's what it looks like. Roommates with no benefits. Have you ever been there? It's an empty shell. I think of that quote by Henry Thoreau, "Leading lives of quiet desperation?" That was us.

We would still be very affectionate publicly, in the sense that we would do certain things together as a family. We spent years where our whole life revolved around the children. We're running around immersed in our children's sports, school activities and recitals.

Both my kids are athletes who compete nationally and provincially, and so, it was very easy to disappear into that. My wife and I worked and there were times we wouldn't see each other till 11:30 at night. By the time our kids were in their mid-teens we looked at each other and said, "What's left for us?" Who are we? What are doing here? How did we get here? The clichés were over the top!

We both knew the answer instantly. There was zero, nada, zilch left. It was at that point that we decided to separate and we spent the next nine months apart. At the end of that time, we knew we needed to decide about the next step and there was something inside the both of us that didn't want it to end. So, we made one of the toughest choices in our lives. To get back together and work on our problems and if you remember from the first chapter that period of honesty between us to clear the air, was one of the most brutal in my life. One truly had to have the balls of steel to make it through.

Starting Over

One of the things that I had decided early in the process was that I needed to introduce WOW into our marriage. In the early days, it was so easy to wow. The gifts came easy, the poetry flowed endlessly and love letters were passed back and forth like a football. Long phone conversations lasting until the early morning hours and usually involving us professing our undying love for one another. Then, when did it all change? It was time to bring that back.

Through it all, however, I knew that in terms of "WOWing," my wife meant that I loved this person no matter what. It did not matter what this person did or had done to me, or I had done to her, I had to let that all go.

Once we had finished that period of therapy, I honestly knew that I wanted to reignite the relationship. So I was very surprised when she told me that she was unsure. We had fixed things in terms of our friendship which was one thing we had needed to do. Even though I had always thought we were friends, my wife had made it very clear during the "honesty therapy," that we were not even close to being friends.

I had spent the better part of 20 years not listening to her, not accepting her ideas and overpowering her decisions.

Even when it came to the children, I felt I knew best. Even simple things like decisions for the house, I would make on my own. I pretty much did everything my own way.

When she reminded me of all those things, I made excuses like, "I had to do it. You're not interested anyway." "You're indifferent," and "You're cold," Then, I came to realize that none of that was the truth. The reality was that she gave up wanting to be my friend because I just didn't listen. I thought I had put her and the children first. I may have put the children first, but I didn't put her first.

After that, it came to a critical point where it was decision time. I simply said, "I love you. I will always love you. I love the children. You and I are always going to be there for one another, Now, I'm telling you that either we work at this now and we agree that this is our relationship for the future, or we agree that we will create lives apart."

There was no doubt in her mind when I also told her, "If we separate, I am going to follow my dream. I will move away, create a new relationship with someone else," that was when she was sure she had to save us! When faced with the realization that we would have to create a new world for the children and that I may not be available 24/7 like I always was in the past, it was clear 'we' were what she wanted.

Sometimes you don't realize what you want until it is going to be taken away for good. I knew that I wanted her to be my wife forever. That was my heart's desire but if she didn't want that, too, I was still going to live a good life. It was then that she realized that she didn't want to let me go either, that she still loved me.

Necessity – an urgency, a basic instinct for survival kicked in. It was decision time. No more waffling. I moved back home again.

That was when I truly started to learn about WOW in a marriage. In the beginning, it was all very innocent, in the sense that we were reigniting our relationship. What I didn't know was that my wife was also suffering from depression and physical problems. She was facing some serious health issues, degradation and arthritis of her neck and problems along her arms and hand.

For someone who had worked her entire life, always retained a job (since she was 15 years old) and had been so independent, these physical ailments caused depression to set in. She had gone through an extremely challenging time, and our separation hadn't helped any. What made it very hard was that I knew nothing about depression. All I thought (mistakenly) was that I have this insane woman in the house with me.

I didn't recognize this person. I didn't know who this person was. I didn't understand her bouts of melancholy, and her bouts of physical pain. When I realized, I could WOW her by supporting her the way she needed, I became aware and learned what I could. I read anything I could to help her. One of the first things we decided to do was go to Paris, France.

That trip really changed our way of thinking. It was what we needed. We had been in our life for so long that we needed to experience something different. We had time to be alone, and share intimate moments. We were living a dream. The little cafes, the espressos, the morning croissants, the walks along the Seine, looking at the architecture and going through churches crated instant WOW. It felt like we were 16-year-olds again, and we came home more in love than ever. It was one of best WOW times of our lives.

Since then, it's just been up, up, up. There hasn't been a day in the last two years that we have not said how much we love each other; how much we care about each other. We show each other every day. When she is at home, every morning she cooks breakfast for me, and we eat breakfast together. Few words, but just together.

Now that I work from home more often than the office, I spend the better part of the day with her. We want to be together all the time. We'll call and text each other all the time, when we are apart just like we did when we were teenagers. I could not see my life without her, even as my friend. I realize now that she is my best friend in the world. How WOW is that?

Here is one important thing that I have learned throughout all of this. You can have a mediocre marriage where you don't really like or understand each other, where you go for years like I did barely surviving.

Or...

You can have a truly extraordinary relationship with your spouse, where you each meet the other's need. Where you not only understand each other, but love and even like each other. It is an incredible place to be. I never knew how wonderful it could be until I experienced it for myself.

But, it does take work. Note, I do not call it hard work. Rather, it takes committed, affectionate, thoughtful, fun work. It is all in the viewpoint. I must choose sometimes to put my needs aside to make sure hers are met. I have had to learn to do things I don't like because it makes her happy. And the truth is the not liking part is something I am creating. I can be with anything, like and enjoy anything. Again, all in the viewpoint. The funny thing is when I do that and I see that beautiful smile and she tells me she loves me, it is more than worth it.

How to WOW Your Spouse

It all comes down to the little things that you do everyday. If you take it all for granted, the relationship will do the same to you. Doing those special things only occasionally, will never yield your WOW results. What are some of those special little things? Let's look at some of them.

First, I believe in **creating an aesthetic space** around you that is beautiful. As an artist, I love to surround myself and my wife with beautiful things. I don't think it is a superficial thing. I believe it is a matter of choosing pieces that are beautiful and meaningful to you and your partner. Items you choose together: like paintings, furnishings. The carpet. The bed.

One of the ways we improved our surroundings was to sell the home we had lived in for 20 years and move into a 2,000-square-foot penthouse by the lake. We have an amazing view of the lake and our beautiful downtown area and we have been WOWed ever since. We took ourselves out of what we knew and got out of the "too-comfortable". We recreated our world! No more suburbs! Been there done that!

Which leads us to idea number two: **don't be afraid to shake things up.** Complacency is death. Start with baby steps. Right after we reignited our relationship, we totally gutted the house. We spent a year renovating the entire house. Floors, dining room, everything was redone, and we loved it.

We finished the space and we did everything together. We picked the furnishings together. We picked the floorings together. Dealing with the workers that made our lives a nightmare for six months only made us stronger.

One year in and we are loving our new lifestyle. I also let my wife take the reign on most of it, because I find that I always overpower her in those decisions. I'm a neat freak, and I'm also very aesthetically inclined. Because I'm a visual guy, I'm an artist, I want everything perfect. Sometimes you should let things go.

Thirdly, I stood by her and the **decisions we made.** We were always a united front, my wife and I never disagreed in front of anybody else or our children. Behind closed doors, we might agree to disagree, and we would work through it, but our children have never seen us argue. The only time was just before I moved out during our separation. The month or two prior to that was a very difficult time indeed. We regret those moments, but now there is rarely a disagreement, even when my kids try to do the teenage thing and attempt to divide and conquer, it never happens.

It drives them crazy. My daughter, who is 20 now, always says, "You and Mom always agree. You never take my side." I reply, "You are right. Your mother and I will never, ever disagree when it comes to you two. Because we love you the same, we want the same things for you, and one will not have a different opinion than the other. We can talk about it and you can try to change our minds, but you'll never see us disagree." It was comically frustrating for them, because no matter how they tried to sneak through with the divisional tactics, we never allowed it to work.

Fourth is understanding the **male and female spirit**. As humans we have both, to some degree. For the most part, obviously, men have way more male spirit and women have way more female spirit. Of course, there are exceptions and a variety of scales in between but at the heart of a male/female relationship there are two such spirits.

For a long time in my marriage, I took on what I consider the female spirit. Meaning, she was working and I was working, but the scales were tipped to the point where I did everything for the kids while she worked certain late hours, when she wasn't home. It's not that housework is just a woman's job, --please don't get me wrong--but somewhere along the line, I ended up taking some of the female energy in the relationship and she took on more of the male spirit. If you do that, you're going to lose that sexual energy that's there between you in the relationship. It's not about sexism or chauvinism. It's about seeing who you truly are.

There are times when women and men both are guilty of flip-flopping, but we're still male and female spirits. You can agree without speaking that, "Okay, I'm going to stay at home, and I'm going to be the stay-at-home dad. You're going to be the mom that works," but trust me when I say, there will be a time where she comes through that door looking for her man, her male spirit partner. It's not about money. It's not about a job. It's not about who's the boss, because my wife and I are very equal on that.

This is not about politics, or government, or equality. It's about your spirit, and the need to respect that spirit. That's when the "WOW" happens. When you realize that, "When my wife comes home, she needs me to be HER man." There's going to be times when I need to be treated like a guy and she needs to be treated like a woman. She wants to be carried. Yes, I mean literally over the threshold, to the bed even just in play. She wants to be protected. She wants to be loved and be taken care of at a certain point, and if she doesn't get that as a female spirit, you're doomed. You're simply doomed. I was, until I learned the truth.

The same thing goes for the man in the relationship. He needs to be respected and treated like a king. He needs to know that his wife wants to be protected by him, and be strong for her. That he is her SAFE place for when she feels weak.

I will make sure that I open the doors for her when I can. I will always drive. She's a great driver, but when we're out, I do the driving. I joke with her because that's when her female spirit comes out. I'll say to her, "You drive. I'm being lazy," and she goes, "No. You drive." It's something she has communicated to me that she does not want to do and it is not just my wife. The other day I was talking to someone about this and she said that while she is a great driver when she is with her husband, he drives 98% of the time and she likes it that way.

In the past, I would say, "Oh, no, you drive." I didn't realize that, "Oh, wait. Here's a moment where I can choose to give in to the female-male spirit." The female spirit is telling me, "Drive. Be the man and take me around." I know it sounds so primitive, but it's the truth. It's what we are. We are male and female energies, and we need to respect that. 98% of the time, I drive, unless it is dangerous for me to do so. For example, long trips where I have done most of the driving and I am about to pass out at the wheel or where I may be ill, but those times are rare.

Number five is **keep up the romance and the trips**. Get away when you can. Buy each other surprises. Spend a little extra on entertainment when you can. It doesn't mean you need to spend all your money. When I say surround yourself by aesthetics and pretty things, I don't mean you need to go out and buy a Picasso. You can certainly go out and buy a nice piece of art, or a nice furnishing, or something special that would make the two of you happy every time you see it.

Local galleries are filled with beautiful work by hungry artists. Street art sales, that you can stroll through together, can yield amazing pieces. New web sites that allow you to custom and personalize furnishings. I have designed my own pillows, mouse pads, posters using my own designs, very cost effectively. It's a wonderful way to add that distinctive touch to your home.

As we look around our house, we both are happy. Why? Because we shared a moment in time, picked that together or fell in love with a piece. We created agreement. It could be a photograph. It could be a frame. It could be a piece of furniture. Surround yourself by the beautiful things that you created together and create a harmonious space.

Sixth, you want to live in a **place of serenity, and peace, and happiness.** One of the things that does it for us is music. Soft music playing when you can. When I come home, there's music playing, candles lit, just to keep me at peace, because she knows I've had a hectic day. At home, when I'm working, she will bring me my lunch. She'll make sure tea's ready for us and we will have it together. These are just moments where we're creating togetherness that we never did before.

֎֍

Hi, it's Raymond here. I want to share with you a seventh way to WOW your spouse. **How to evaluate the value of a gift you are giving.** My formula for that is perceived value to the recipient divided by the actual cost to the giver. Let's say I give you a $20 bill. The perceived value to the recipient is $20 and the cost to the giver is $20. When you divide $20 by $20 you get one. So, one is the midway point, anything better than one is good and anything less than one is bad.

Let me give you another example. Say I give you a Starbuck's card for $20. That's not worth $20 to you because you may not like Starbucks, or you might be on a diet, or Starbucks might be out of your way. You can also buy $20 Starbucks cards on EBay for $17. So, if you divide 17 by 20 it is .85. Less than one. If you give someone a gift they can't use at all, the value number is zero.

On the other end, maybe you made something for someone and you put a lot of time and effort into it. The person loved it and displayed it in the home. The materials may have only cost you $20 but in the recipient's eyes, it is worth $500. Now, your value number goes up to 25, which is very high.

When it comes to your spouse, it is very important to know what they value as a gift. You may spend $500 on something they hate because you think it has value or $5 on something they absolutely love and love you for it. Don't assume that you know. Ask your spouse what they like and then give it to them, whenever you can.

What Do You Want Most?

Everyone has priorities in life. Even when you think that you don't, you do. Is your spouse one of them? If you want a WOW marriage, then your spouse must be one of the highest priorities you have.

Every day, you must make the choice to WOW your spouse. Every day, you must study your spouse and find out the things that please them and then do it. I know that my marriage changed when we both focused on WOWing each other.

The other thing that naturally happens is that others are WOWed as well. The healthier your relationship is with your spouse, the more that you can help others. You become a positive influence in this world, starting with the most precious gift that you have in life--your children. That is what we are going to focus on in the next chapter.

CHAPTER 3

How to Develop WOW With Your Kids

Ash`s Discernment

*"All children are artists.
The problem is how to remain an artist
once they grow up."*

—Pablo Picasso

Kids are one of our most valuable treasures in life. No book on WOW would be complete without discussing them. One of the ways we can change the world is by teaching the next generation the power of WOW in their lives.

Unfortunately, most children grow up in an unWOW world. I've seen kids fall to drugs and alcohol when there is no WOW in their life. They grow up feeling that there's no future for them. Many times, that message comes straight from day one, from the way a parent didn't choose to show them love.

When there's un-WOW at home on a daily basis, I've seen children bring that un-WOW out at school. The child is out of control in class, has absolutely no filter, or thinks it's perfectly all right to bully and swear. These are all signs of unWOW in their life. When no one is reminding them of how special they are, when no one's telling them that they can do almost anything, how can you expect them to be at their best?

Another sign is loss of communication. They cut communication because they have no reason to want to communicate. They feel self-conscious and insecure about their own lives and they cut people off. They think it's because of what other people do to them. They have a victim mentality. But truthfully, they isolate themselves, because they can't deal with their own emotions.

As these children grow into adulthood, they follow the path of mediocrity. There's no WOW in it. There may be the occasional moments of WOW if they are lucky, like getting married or having children. But unless they have someone that shows up in their life who is inspirational or someone who has given them a glimpse of what they can achieve, they will spend their time wishing and wanting the better things in life but ending up angry, disappointed and bitter. They don't understand the mindset of WOW to be able to achieve it.

Qualities Kids With WOW Possess

Kids with WOW inside will have a powerful sense of independence. They have a well-developed sense of confidence, and a powerful sense of being able to control their future. More than anything, this sense of autonomy, that they can control their future in any way they want is the key to them becoming anything they want to be.

The funny thing is, they're not always politically correct. They're not always the politest kids, because they will say what's on their mind and they're independent thinkers.

They're not afraid to go against the establishment, but they do it in a productive, positive way. We're not talking about someone that's going to graffiti up the sides of the school or burn the school down in protest. These are the children you'll see making a difference in their world at an early age. Taking action and caring about others, while their peers are watching TV, playing video games or being on Facebook.

These kids, they're not always the ones that have the best marks, but they're always the ones that are doing well in the courses they care about. If they're able to choose the road and route they want to go, they find a way to excel.

Some other attributes you will see is that they are highly creative, energetic and generally very positive. They do well in sports and other extra-curricular activities, in fact they tend to do well in most things. That doesn't mean that kids that struggle in school can't be WOW kids. WOW comes from the heart, and if a child truly tries in life, that is WOW.

My kids were never the top students, but they were always among the most positive, popular, happy, loved and liked in school and everybody knew them. Yes, early on, my daughter got high marks and was a top athlete. My son too, enjoyed similar successes, but it's not always about marks, it's about their voice and their ability to influence others.

In my opinion, WOW kids work smart, not hard. They work diligently, they work confidently, they contribute. Other kids seek them out, to complete the task. They're always the ones leading charge of the project and occasionally will come home frustrated because they had to do everybody else's work. Teachers love them because they relate well to adults and children.

One of the things I love about WOW kids is their ability to be polite and kind. More than that, they're able to speak to adults in a respectful, yet equal way. Kids that have WOW in their lives, that are achieving WOW even early on, can relate to people of all ages, not just people their age. WOW kids tend to be very good with other kids. They are tomorrow's leaders, educators and teachers.

5 Ways to Develop WOW in Your Kids

While there may be the occasional, rare child that naturally has some WOW qualities, most kids develop them as they grow, through their parents instilling key virtues in them.

As a parent, you must be willing to invest the time and effort into your kids so they learn from an early age how to live a WOW life. It's a long-term commitment, where you won't see the end results sometimes until they are well into adulthood. There will be rewards along the way as you see your children grow in it, but there is a sweetness that comes when you watch your adult kids succeed.

So, how do you develop WOW in your kids? Let's look at some of the easy things you can do each day.

How to Develop WOW With Your Kids

1. The Words You Speak

There has never been a day that I did not tell my child, in some form or another that I love them, that I miss them, that they're incredible. Ever since my children were infants, I can remember changing their diapers and looking into their eyes and saying, "You are beautiful. You are outstanding. You are extraordinary and your father adores you."

Now, as they got older, I would still tell them I love them. As they got out of the car (because I drove them everywhere) I would say, "Tell me everything that happens later. Make a difference, achieve your best!" I wanted to make sure that they would leave my presence with a positive message to carry through the day.

2. How You Handle Disagreement

We have never had a disagreement that we couldn't get past. We have always talked things out and 30 seconds later, we were in each other's arms. It was always a priority to keep communication open and listen to each other with an open heart.

3. Age Appropriate Independence

We allowed our kids to learn how to make choices from a young age. As they got older they were allowed to make more and more decisions. The key to this concept is allowing them to make decisions when they are ready to accept the consequences of that decision.

For example, we didn't allow our kids to get piercings and tattoos. Those are decisions that you cannot easily reverse, so they needed to be mature enough to live with their choices.

4. Lots of Creative Activity

When they were small children, we would do everything together. I would take them to libraries and read books to them. We would go on treasure hunts, we would create fun games. I would make sure they had creative outlets. Both children studied music, from a very early age, and were able to choose whatever instrument they wanted to play. They were also permitted to choose their own sports.

My son ultimately went into swimming for two years and then he chose to go into jump rope, where he has competed nationally. He is ranked as one of Canada's top competitors and competes internationally as well. My daughter was a swimmer for nine years, competitively and then she went on to instruct swimming, and was a lifeguard for several years. Now she is training to be a paramedic.

Our kids, while still in their teens, lived these extraordinary lives because they have the capacity to reach for further horizons. They have that capacity because we taught them how to set goals. We taught them to go after the things they want to achieve. They are living a life of WOW. Imagine how exciting it is, how affirming it is, when you, a teenager, are competing in Paris, France, for the World Jump Rope Championship, meeting people from all over the world?

Or my daughter, who has had the opportunity to swim competitively across Canada. She has learned to save lives early on and now she shares her knowledge, teaching young kids. Consider how proud she must be when she hears from other parents, "You make such a difference to my child. My child wants to come swimming because you teach her;" she can believe it and continue to do more and more.

5. Be Involved in Family Decisions

Another way to develop WOW in your kids is make sure they are involved in decisions. Where you move, what house you buy, when you go shopping, in all kinds of circumstances. Give them some choices of what they want. They must have fruits and vegetables, but let them pick them out.

Have them contribute to choices in the house, when you're designing things. Even when they're young. Let them choose their bedrooms, their colors and their art. Give them lots of choice, because that will empower them. Let them know that they're contributing.

Most children are constantly told what to do, have things done for them, and as such have no sense of contribution. What is the result? They end up feeling left out and unable to contribute WOW within their families. They begin to think, "What's the point? You're not going to listen to me. You don't know what I want. I'm just going to do what I want." What do you want your kids to say?

My kids continue to want to spend time with my wife and me to this day. They want to go on vacations, they want to go to dinner, they want to have fun with us. We enjoy them more and more as they develop into adulthood, too. They are growing into interesting, inspiring, WOW people!

The Results of Raising WOW Kids

The biggest results you will see from raising WOW kids is seeing them grow into passionate, engaged adults. They love to spend time together as a family when they are adults. Instead of withdrawing, or moving away from you mentally, emotionally and physically, they draw close to you.

The four of us go for a spa day, getting manicures and pedicures together. It's quite funny. Some families go out camping and hiking together; my kids and I like to go get our nails done together. It doesn't really matter what you do, you can have all your family fun favourites.

We love to vacation together. We always make it fun. My 20-year-old daughter and my 17-year-old son still will jump into bed with us on a Saturday morning if they're home, and talk about what we'll do for the day. We love it when they do that.

Then that trickles its way over to other children. Their friends want to be part of the family. You know that you have WOW kids when they are proud to "show off" their parents! There has never been a time where my kids have ever made my wife and I feel like we must stay away from their friends. They want us to be at their parties. They want us to be at their shows, and their sporting events. If I'm busy, my children immediately ask, "Why aren't you going to come?" They have come to expect us to be interested and engaged in their lives. That's when you know that you've achieved the WOW, when we're not seen as a burden to them. We're not an inconvenience to their plans. They want us to be a part of their life.

It doesn't matter how old your kids are. Even if they are adults, it is never to late for you to start showing them WOW in their life. Make that connection and build that bridge. Give them opportunities to WOW you and then when they do, make sure that you recognize, appreciate and reward them for it. You will be so glad you did.

Have you enjoyed this book so far? If you have, would you do me a favour? If you got it on Amazon or some other online book site, would you go and leave a review? Every review helps others to know that this book will have a positive effect on their life.

Now in the next chapter we are going to look at how you expand that WOW out to the rest of your family and friends. The effects of WOW just keep growing.

CHAPTER 4

How to Keep Your Friends & Family Close With The Power of WOW

Ash`s Insight

"The family is one of nature's masterpieces."
—George Santayana

Just before we get into talking about extended family and friends, I want to share an important concept with you: and that is the Light Emitting Ripple Effects of WOW. When you look at light rays, they expand out from the point of origin to encompass everything. Your life of WOW should do the same thing.

It starts with a feeling of connection to the universe and an understanding that you were created for a reason. Then, by knowing who you are you can take the best of yourself and use it to influence others and to create a better world.

As we influence others, they receive and take in the good and that empowers them to reach out to others and so on. It has the same effect as the random acts of kindness movement. When good is done to you, you want to share it with others, and so on.

But, Wondrous Outstanding Worth is way more powerful then just one single act of kindness. WOW changes people's entire lives because it changes you from the inside out. Lasting change in this world will only happen as people's hearts are renewed; actions alone are not enough.

Everything starts with you. Work on *you* as the point of origin. Make sure you continue to WOW yourself, mentally, physically, and spiritually. Without a solid core within yourself, you cannot be a help or a WOW to anybody else.

Light cannot emanate outwards if there isn't enough light. You can make the motions, but it's all for naught if you continue with that "self esteem issue," hide that drinking problem, or think that food addiction is anything else but an addiction. It is easy to put yourself second, but doing so is really an unWOW, not just to you but to everyone else in your life. The basic structure of Light Emanation depends on WOWing yourself so there is enough WOW to spread around. Only after you have done this self-WOW work, can you cause the next trickle effect: to your family.

Now, we have already covered the first levels of family, your spouse and your children. They are the most important people to focus on and those relationships are where you will see the greatest results. There is nothing more rewarding in life than to watch your family not only experiencing WOW, but then sharing it with others.

From there, WOW moves outward to your extended family and friends. That is what we look at in this chapter. For WOW to reach the world, you must share WOW in each area of your life.

Let's take a moment here to explain that even the best WOW can be undervalued by the person receiving it. We think of it as a "giving your pearls to swine". Pigs will eat anything, including garbage. They do not care about too much beyond eating and sleeping. They can be covered in mud and manure, but if their bellies are full, nothing else matters.

So, if you place something valuable in front of pigs, such as pearls, the pigs will either eat them, because they don't know what they are, or ignore them, because the pearls aren't food, or get mad at you because you aren't giving them what they want to eat. They want garbage, not pearls.

Sometimes, people with whom you try to share WOW will behave the same way. *(Before you start sending me emails demanding, "How dare you call the people I know and love pigs !?!" I AM NOT.)* Let me explain.

Not everyone in life is ready to receive and give WOW. Maybe they were never taught the concept or maybe, it was literally beaten out of them in childhood. Maybe life has been so hard that they can't see WOW even if it is right in front of their face. All they know is the garbage that is placed in front of them everyday and they are too afraid to even think of anything else. They will even fight you for their right to live a life of unWOW!

So, the question becomes what do you do with your extended family and friends who want nothing to do with the love and excellence you portray in your life? For the most part, you simply let them be. Love them anyway, and when given opportunities, plant seeds in their life and wait for them to grow.

The important thing is to take the time to analyze each situation you go into and act accordingly. If you walk into a room and you are the happiest, most positive person there and everyone else is miserable, then you can still be happy on the inside, but tone it down a bit on the outside, so people feel more comfortable with you. Be considerate and share WOW on a level they can handle. Bring it in the way that they can understand you; share WOW in a way that means something to them.

This also allows you to share their space, meet them at their unWOW level and then increase that to more of a WOW. You can do that by first matching their emotional attitude and then consciously work them up. At these times, the best WOW you can give is a sympathetic ear and, if it seems welcome, a comforting response.

WOWing Others Means WOWing Yourself First

When my business partner and I decided to close the men's clothing shop, we started a millwork/carpentry business where we designed and built kitchen fixtures and wedding decorations. I was exhausted.

During the day, I was selling products to "bride-zillas" and marketing to interior design firms. Then, I would work in the carpentry shop evenings until 3 am, helping to make products like the ones I had sold that day. I wasn't very good at it. Carpentry was never my strong suit as my former business partner can attest. Misery, unhappiness and anger were fast becoming my best friends and it was affecting my relationships at home.

The Catalyst That Changed My Life

During this period, I received a call from a friend asking me to take part in a career day for a Grade Five class. I decided to do it and I am so glad that I did. I spent an hour talking about what I do and talking about being true to yourself, following your dreams, making sure that you can achieve it, and I was lying. I was a hypocrite in front of these children because I was miserable.

I had convinced myself that I was in business and creating the future I wanted, but nothing could be further from the truth. So, I walked out of that classroom and, on the same day, quit my partnership with my oldest friend, a friendship that had lasted 30 years. My partner was not surprised, as he saw how unhappy I was, although he was somewhat saddened at the thought that for us, it was the end of an era. Thankfully, we have remained friends. I will always love him, without question. But, I had no idea what I was going to do– none. It seemed I was starting from scratch, without a lot of options before me.

I was 30 and so computer illiterate that I didn't even know how to save a file on my desktop. Within a week, I signed up for art and graphic design courses at a well-known college. It was daunting going back to school after ten years. I overcame all my fears because this was a "do-or-die" time, yet again. But, necessity overcomes any obstacles. I knew that I was starting to follow a path that was true to my heart, and that decision has led me to all the true success that I've ever had.

You can't lead others to WOW, if you don't have it or live it yourself.

WOWing Your Parents

As I was thinking about this chapter of the book, I came to realize that there needed to be a separate section on how you WOW different types of people in your extended family and friends, especially your parents. Each group is different, and if you want to have the most impact, you must take that into consideration.

I spent many years in a very negative relationship with my father. My parents were divorced when I was 16. It was a turbulent time and our relationship was unhealthy. I can say now that he was a good man, and he loved my brother, my mother and I unconditionally, but he did not know how to be a father and he did not know how to be a husband.

He was born into a world of privilege in East Africa. Then, back in 1972, when I was just a child, Idi Amin took over and kicked us out of the country. My father was wealthy: he had property, servants, a car dealership, and money. Overnight, our wealth was taken away from us. Now we were refugees in a country that was not our own, relying on others for our basic needs. That displacement and loss had a profound mental effect on my father.

In the early seventies, a man like my father would not even consider going for psychoanalysis and therapy. We didn't have the term "depression" in our culture until much later. He was suffering, and we suffered because of that.

It took many years, but I came to realize that my father was the most amazing man he could be with the tools he had. When I had that insight, it was a WOW moment for me that allowed me to be with him, and love him. I could treat him with respect, welcome him back into my home and WOW him like I never had before.

When I opened my heart to give him WOW, we could have closure and reunite. I was able to see him with my children. He was a brilliant grandfather. My families' memories of my father are only positive. They can't imagine him being anything other than the kind, loving man they knew him to be, let alone the angry, hurtful and verbally abusive man he once was.

It was never a physically abusive relationship. He was never physically abusive to me, my mother and my brother, but verbally and emotionally, it was another story. It was not healthy, but that all changed. When I spread WOW to him and accepted him, he WOWed me by being the most amazing grandfather he could be. My kids benefited from that. I even remember sitting there one day watching him with my kids thinking, "Who the hell is this man? He's not the same man who raised me!"

I took all the blame out of what happened in our relationship. I took ownership for the fact that the bond we created had not happened earlier on. I took responsibility (NOT BLAME) for what I had created with him. That was the key to the shift.

This is how WOW spreads. Once I accepted him, once we had closure for the past and we accepted our faults and our weaknesses, a WOW love grew. He was always fun, and I saw him only in a positive light. From that day forward, I have never said, when asked about my dad, "Yeah, well, we were estranged. He was okay. We had a tough go, etc." Etc.

Now I tell people, "He was a great man. He was loving and kind. We had a tough go in the beginning. We came as refugees, but he made good and he did the best he could with what he had." That is how WOW changed my life with my father.

WOW, for me, means taking full responsibility for the relationship. It is about showing up, even if it is hard to see it from that vantage point. You are creating that relationship with your parent, good or bad. It is hard for most people to accept.

My mother was always my rock. Solid and reliable, just a super mom, loving immensely and without ever looking for anything in return. She raised my brother and me on her own. She instilled WOW in me from an early age because she was so kind and giving. She never said, "I love you," with the hopes of ever hearing it back ... she just said it wholly out of love and acceptance.

She was the first person that showed me how to WOW other people. She had an unconditional love for humanity, period. I remember thinking, *this woman will do anything for anybody*. Ultimately, my Dad did, too, and there are notable examples of how WOW can spread to your community and then nations.

When my Dad died, I went to his funeral and there were a thousand people there. That in itself was a WOW moment even for me! What did this man do to inspire such a turnout? Now as the firstborn, I was standing at the head of the line and greeted the procession of family members, relatives, and friends. Every person that walked up, would shake my hand and say, "Your Dad was an angel. He was the most beautiful person I've ever met. He gave and gave."

I remember looking at my brother and thinking, *Who is this man they are talking about? They cannot be talking about my dad!* They would regale me with stories of the WOW things he did, like going out at 2:00 in the morning to help the neighbors start their car; giving rides to single mothers in the building where he lived because they were struggling with their relationships with their children; and helping and feeding friends and family. He always knew the best places to eat!

So, how do you WOW your parents? You love, honour and respect them. You make them a part of your family's life. You recognize as I did, that they did the best they could with what they had. You forgive and forget their mistakes and then WOW them with so much honour, that it changes not only their lives, but others' lives as well. Let go of the past. It will only eat away at your WOW.

WOW means closing the past disharmony with your parents once and for all because all of us start with incomplete relationships with our parents. Start there. Complete the cycles that are open with them and the unfinished words spoken. End the cycle, the pattern with them so as not to take the unWOWs into your future relationships, whether with others or your children. Approach it from a place of empowerment and responsibility, not blame. Again not always easy but so necessary if you want to have WOW in your future.

Even if it means accepting that you can't be best friends, have closure for yourself without the bitterness. You control that, they do not. You are the ruler and creator of your world - not them. The actions of others does not dictate how you react to them. You do. Choose to be helpless, sad or angry or choose to accept, acknowledge, and move on. Or you can simply complain to every person you meet for the next 20 years about the injustice your parents caused. The choice, the viewpoint is yours to command.

What About The In-Laws?

They are important, too! WOWing my in-laws means always making them part of our family so that my wife has and continues to have a strong relationship with them. A lot of people take their in-laws for granted. They may or may not have patience and understanding for the people that have raised their spouse. But for me, I love my in-laws because they raised my wife, and they raised her to be the most loving and affectionate woman I adore.

Why wouldn't I respect them? I'm always making sure that I greet them with terms of respect and act inside the ways of their culture. I make sure I go and visit them as often as I can. I make our time together worth something. We laugh and joke and have fun, and I create a WOW atmosphere when I visit. They know that when Ash is over, he's the jovial, happy guy. They're in their eighties, and they want to make sure that their only daughter will truly be looked after when they've gone. It is a cultural code and it gives them peace to know that they can rely on me.

How to Have WOW Relationships With Your Siblings

The one relationship where I have struggled the most is my relationship with my brother. You must know when WOW is enough for a certain person. For example, my brother and I have never been very close. As a kid, I was always trying to be way too cool. He wouldn't hang out with me. I was always the popular guy. He was always more studious, and quiet. He was more introverted. We didn't have the closest relationship. I was always the loud, obnoxious "life of the party", and he was always the quiet "homebody".

We didn't have a lot in common, but we loved each other. When we were young, we used to fight often, but as we grew older, a mutual respect and love has grown between us. We have a relationship where we may not talk every day, or even call to just say, "Let's hang out." But I know that he and I will always be there for one another. Whenever we needed each other, we were there. We're a call away. No questions asked. He's a proven support system for me and me for him.

We created WOW in our relationship because we can trust each other. Do we have a relationship where we hang out on weekends or travel together or even where are our spouses/partners are close with each other, no? But he loves my kids. He's the best possible uncle when he sees them. He's very much like my father--where when he comes to visit, they adore him. They don't see him all the time, but whenever they do, it is always a WOW experience. That is the extent of the WOW that I can create with him. It's comfortable for him. I love him—full stop. He has never been one for getting overly sentimental or teary, and that is totally ok. In fact, he will probably even laugh at me once he reads this book! He will say, "Yep, just like Ash." But anything more would be uncomfortable for him. When it comes to WOW, you can offer it, but not every person is going to receive it. Be fine with that knowledge. That is a WOW in and of itself.

Let them receive the WOW to the point that they're able to handle. WOWing somebody is not pushy. WOWing somebody is not showing off. WOWing somebody is not going in and doing all these over the top things for people in the hopes that you're going to get some reciprocal love. It's always about giving without putting expectations on another person, because you know that the WOW will come back to you in other ways.

It is accepting everyone as truly beautiful creatures, yes everyone, and yes that too is sometimes hard for most people. I love people, and I try to come to any new relationship with nothing but "this person is amazing," just like I am.

When you are dealing with your extended family, WOW means love. Many times, the people you are closest to speak a different love language than you. So, it is important to recognize that and communicate WOW in a way they can understand. A terrific book that discusses this concept more fully is *The Five Love Languages* by Gary Chapman.

And finally . . .

WOWing Your Friends

WOWing your friends, that's simple. It's loving my friends and accepting them for who they are, 100%, as well as accepting their families for who they are and their children as well. It's accepting without judgment and it's certainly accepting without competing. Take the competition out of it. We spend our whole lives trying to keep up with the Joneses and from that, we lose affinity for one another. I have been there and I have been guilty of it.

Simple gestures, like making sure I answer a text in a reasonable amount of time is a WOW. I don't care who you are, people that don't respond to texts within a reasonable amount of time, meaning an hour or even two hours, unless there's some real emergency or they're traveling on a plane, simply are saying they don't really care to honour that person with a response.

Of course, there are extenuating circumstances, perhaps you are driving or in a meeting that lasts too long but, for the most part, you just know when you are not honouring someone with a reply and ensuring that when you are not held up by those extenuating circumstances any longer, you immediately share the why with them.

People say, "Well, I'm so busy." What I've come to learn is that you make time for the things you want to and, outside of that, you just choose not to make time. I don't believe people when they say they were too busy. There's no such thing. You make time for what you want.

I make sure my friends know that I love them. I make sure that we're together for holidays. I make sure that there's affinity when we're together. I remember their birthdays when I can, and always belatedly where possible. I remember what they love. I remember their favorite things. I remember their children's loves. I make sure they know they can tell me anything and that I will always have their back.

In short, I make sure that I am a part of their lives.

I am excited for the next section of this book as we take WOW into the world of business. It is one of the passions in my life and I can't wait to share with you the WOW concepts that have made my professional life extraordinary.

SECTION 2

Applying WOW to Your Professional Life

CHAPTER 5

How to WOW Your Employer Into Raises And Promotions

Ash's Knowledge

"If I create from the heart, nearly everything works: if from the head, almost nothing."
—Marc Chagall

Even though I have spent most of my life as an entrepreneur, there were a few years where I worked for other people. One, sticks out in particular.

The first time I left my businesses and I was starting a new career from scratch, it was daunting. Thankfully, I had some connections and one was the owner of some printing stores.

I wanted to "WOW" him in my interview, so I said, "There's nothing I can't do. Because I've been in business for myself, I can treat your business like it is my own. I can look at things from an owner's perspective, not just from an employee's perspective. I can open the books and see where the problem areas lie. I can engage customers, I can market, I can talk to customers, and I can sell. There's no part of the business that I can't address, simply because I've done it all inside my own businesses since I was fifteen years old." And he hired me.

Within a week, I had found discrepancies in the books. It turned out that the manager was taking money for himself and fudging the books to cover it.

When you work for someone else, it is an exchange in WOW. Make it a relationship in which you provide abundance to your company, your immediate supervisors and your clients. You give, and then you give more. You take the initiative. You care more about getting things done and pitch in when someone needs help. It's a little more time, a little more attention, maybe a couple of extra hours. Something that shows him that you're committed. You may think that some of these things are the norm; of course, one does these things. But, you'd be surprised how many people don't get it and, so, these are WOWs.

It's not an intentional, "I want you to notice me" attention-seeking, kind of act, but rather, at the heart of it, based on the feeling that I want to do an excellent job. I want to make sure that I make an impression. I want to help your customers and I want to help myself. It's about making sure I communicate exactly my desires for the future. What I'm looking for. What I want. And making sure everybody is on the same page.

In terms of raises and promotions, I guess the biggest thing for me is that I never set out to do that; they just happened.

I didn't do all these things to get raises and promotions. I did these things so that the company could become the best it could be. That is the essential thing about WOWing your boss, it happens when you are acting with the right motives at heart.

I am going to show you 38 ways to WOW your boss, but a warning: if the only reason you are doing these things is to get noticed and get ahead yourself, then that is simply manipulation. Yes, you will probably get raises and promotions, but in the end, it can be very transparent. The day will come when someone will out-manipulate you and you will be miserable.

On the other hand, when your true motive is to genuinely help your company and put its interest first, these things will come to you and they won't be able to be taken away.

38 Ways to WOW Your Boss

I highly suggest that you incorporate as many of these suggestions into your work ethic as possible. The more you make them a part of your professional demeanor, the more valuable you become to your boss and the more likely raises and promotions will come your way.

1. Become the Go-To Person

Make yourself valuable by being the person that everyone can come to for answers. Even when you might not have the answer right away, be willing to help others by finding the information needed.

2. Always Meet Your Deadlines

Be the person that your boss can rely on to get things done on time. When you can't make the deadline, take responsibility for it by not making excuses and get it done as quickly as possible.

3. Always Respect Your Boss

This one may be difficult, because you may feel that your boss has not earned this respect. Give it anyway. Think of it as respecting the position, boss, until you can respect the person. Respect has the power to change lives. It is an amazing gift that you can give to another person. It shows you value them as a human being and it has a way of getting into another person's heart.

4. Always Make Your Boss Look Good

I know that this may sound counter-intuitive to reaching your goals and dreams, but if you help your boss look good, he/she will remember that, and in the proper time your actions will be rewarded.

When you are being publicly recognized, find a way to thank your boss for their help. Sometimes, let your boss take credit for your ideas. Tell his boss how much you appreciate him and how he helps you to become a better employee. All these things will make your boss feel appreciated.

5. Come Up With Ideas Your Boss Can Use

Intentionally come up with great ideas that your boss can use and claim as his own. Let him shine and be content to watch it happen.

6. Mentor Other People

When your boss sees that you are willing and capable of leading others without asking for extra pay, that will be in your favour. When it comes time for promotions you will have already shown leadership skills and the ability to put the company's needs over your own.

7. Stay Out of the Drama

There are people in every workplace who love to create drama and cause heartache for everyone else. The best thing you can do is to never get involved.

Most people who create the drama have a victim mentality and will at first use, then abuse anyone who allows themselves to get involved. At first, it may seem wonderful that this person really needs you, but over time, your "assistance" will grow more and more to the point where you end up doing their job. Or, you may do damage to your own reputation for always taking their side.

When you try to pull away and get them to take responsibility for their own life, you will be viciously attacked as the other person makes everyone else believe that you are against them. It is just not worth it. The best way to stay out of it is to see it coming and never get involved.

8. Be Willing to Take Small Advances

Most people aren't content to take small promotions, they only want the big ones. Many times, bosses are looking to see how committed you are to the company and by being willing to work with what the company is willing to give you, you show them your worth.

Don't complain about small raises and promotions. Be thankful and grateful and let your boss know that you appreciate what he has done for you.

9. Have a Long-Term Plan

This ties in with number eight, if the company you work for is a good one, then be willing to be in it for the long haul. Have a personal plan that you can work on over the course of five years that allows for upward movement and company growth.

10. Don't Be a Suck Up

Nobody likes someone who is always kissing up to them with flattery that you know is being said to garner favour. There is nothing wrong with complimenting and praising your boss if it is deserved, but keep it truthful and don't do it all the time.

11. Don't Try to Take Over For Your Boss

It is more than okay to come along side of your boss and help him with things that he is doing. It is another thing to try and go behind his back, do his job and try to do it better than him, to show those above him that you want his job.

12. Do Things That Make Your Company Look Great

Everything you do should be done with excellence, so that the client says, "WOW!" Go above and beyond what is expected, give that little bit extra whenever possible. Let the client know that you value him choosing your company over the competition.

13. Act Appropriately

When you are dealing with a client, everything you do reflects on your employer. Don't be rude and crude. While some people say that it is only to be expected, many people do not know where the line of class and etiquette are and cross it. So, consider carefully your language because improper communication for the most part, makes you look unprofessional. While some people are okay with swearing, you would be surprised how many people judge you negatively for it. Good language skills always will reflect well on you and your company.

14. Consistent Action

A great quote on consistency comes from Dale Calvert, "Consistent effort doesn't always create consistent results, but it always creates success." Producing consistent, reliable results at work will not always reap you an immediate harvest, but when your employer is looking to promote someone, you will be given higher consideration over someone who only occasionally gets the job done on time.

If they see that your output is always greater and of a higher quality than your peers' work, you will get the job over the person who only gets results when they think someone is watching or a promotion/raise is coming up. Being consistent shows that you care about the company and that your employer's goals are important to you.

15. Good Attitude

Too simple, right? But it is often overlooked. Do you come into work and grumble and complain all the time? Are people always asking you "What's wrong?" and when you answer, "Nothing," they reply, "Well your face doesn't know it!" People want to be around other people who are positive even when times are hard; people want to be with people who can find the good in any situation. If you are constantly negative, don't be surprised when you are passed over for raises and promotions or even being invited to a colleague's birthday lunch!

16. Dress with WOW

No matter what your position, be sure to dress for the occasion. Even if you work in a factory, at least come in with clean clothes and shower, so no one should have to smell your body odor. If you are unsure about what to wear, then you are better to overdress. Let me give you an example:

My editor's son, Daniel, was looking for his first job and had gotten an interview as a dish washer. She encouraged him to look his best, so he arrived at the interview wearing a full suit and tie. The owner was so impressed that he told Daniel to be at work on Monday at 9am to start his new job. He didn't even interview him.

17. Act Like a Leader

A leader is a person who is willing to go where others are not. A leader takes responsibility for their actions and creates results. A leader sees the best in other people and encourages them to do their best. Demonstrate those skills in your work life and you will be rewarded for them.

A leader also keeps their staff happy and feeling appreciated. A thank-you note for working late every day for a week or a month; acknowledging a work anniversary with flowers or a card; allowing people to telecommute or leave early for something special without complaint – these too are all WOWs. Order lunch-in for your team (no talking about work while eating if agreed unless of course it is a working lunch BUT know the difference) and other small tokens of appreciation will keep people motivated to do their best.

18. Intrapreneurial

One of the things that got me ahead when I was working was my *intrapreneurial* spirit. What's an intrapreneur? Even though I was an employee, I thought like an owner and did everything I could to build the business, even above and beyond my normal responsibilities.

I worked on ways to make the business grow and thrive and it was recognized and rewarded.

19. Address Issues Privately

Every company has issues and problems that need to be solved. The way you approach these issues shows a lot about your character. Always be a solution finder, and never present a problem without having a game plan to fix it. If you have issues with other employees, don't talk to everyone about it.

When it is appropriate and possible, solve the problem on your own. Bosses love learning about problems after they have been solved. If you must involve management, only talk to the right level of management about it. When presenting the problem, don't do so in an accusatory manner, but simply state the facts, without adding opinion to it. Always include the individual(s) concerned with the issue in the discussion when the time comes. Have integrity. Be ready to stand on your convictions, and do not go behind someone's back.

I love this story about Socrates and RUMOURS:

In ancient Greece (469 - 399 BC), Socrates was widely lauded for his wisdom. One day, the great philosopher came upon an acquaintance who ran up to him excitedly and said, "Socrates, do you know what I just heard about one of your students?"

"Wait a moment," Socrates replied. "Before you tell me, I'd like you to pass a little test. It's called the Test of Three."

"Three?"

"That's right, Socrates continued. "Before you talk to me about my student let's take a moment to test what you're going to say. The first test is Truth. Have you made absolutely sure that what you are about to tell me is true?"

No," the man said, "Actually, I just heard about it."

"All right," said Socrates. "So, you don't really know if it's true or not."

"Now, let's try the second test, the test of Goodness. Is what you are about to tell me about my student something good?"

"No, on the contrary ... "

"So," Socrates continued, "You want to tell me something bad about him even though you're not certain it's true?"

The man shrugged, a little embarrassed.

Socrates continued. "You may still pass though, because there is a third test - the filter of Usefulness. Is what you want to tell me about my student going to be Useful to me?"

"No, not really . . . "

"Well," concluded Socrates, "if what you want to tell me is neither True nor Good nor even Useful, why tell it to me at all?"

The man was defeated and ashamed. This was the reason Socrates was a great philosopher and held in such high esteem.

20. Be Willing to Admit Mistakes

Part of taking responsibility is being able to admit when you are wrong and then fix it. By doing this, it shows that you can handle bigger jobs because you won't put the blame on other people when mistakes are made and that you will work to fix errors to the client's satisfaction.

21. Always Do What You Say You Are Going to Do

Keep your word. If you tell a client that you are going to add a little something special to their order, you better make sure you do. With today's technology, there is no reason to forget to do it. Every time you keep your word, you WOW them even more.

22. Don't Skip The Annual Party

Bosses want to know that their employees can handle social situations with grace and charm. WOW them by being a team player. Attend company events, such as parties and celebrations to get to know your boss outside of the work environment. You don't need to be the last to leave, or even the first to arrive. But please avoid the drinking and dancing on tables.

23. Don't Do Things Just to Be Rewarded

Always keep your motives pure. Do your work well, because it benefits the company, not because you benefit from it.

24. Be Helpful

When you are done your own work, don't just sit there doing nothing—ask someone else if they can use your help. This not only demonstrates leadership skills, but shows that you are not going to waste the company's money by sitting around doing nothing. Although with any true production, one's real work flow should never really stop.

25. Do Work Above Your Level

If you want to be promoted to a certain position that is currently open, start to do related duties on top of your regular work. Show your boss that you can handle it, and you will be promoted by default because you are already doing it! Just make sure that taking on those responsibilities is appropriate – volunteer, don't just take over. Also, coming up with recommendations that make things better show that you are a positive thinker who only wants the best for the company. This also shows the *"intrapreneurial"* spirit I spoke of earlier. Make your contribution unique and perhaps in a way that the owner/boss has never considered.

26. Work Hard But Smart

Most employees do not have a decent work ethic. They do the minimum amount to make sure that they get paid and the occasional raise. Do the opposite. Work hard but smartly. Get the job done, don't waste time. Take your work seriously. All these things will get you noticed.

27. Integrity

Never cheat the company of anything. Be honest. Don't steal, not even a paperclip. Don't be willing to "fudge" things. If you act with integrity, your boss will know that he can trust you with more. Don't use lame excuses because you need to leave early. Take responsibility for your own mistakes and correct them quickly.

28. Be Self-Motivated

Don't wait for the boss to tell you to get to work. Always be working. When your work is done, find other things to do.

29. Stay Organized

Always know what is going on, or have access to that information at a moment's notice. Keep your work area tidy. Show that you care how your area looks to others. Bring an extra copy of something to meetings or have it open on your tablet.

30. Be a Great Listener & Ask Great Questions

Listening is often an overlooked skill. If you are unsure of something, don't talk, listen. This reminds me of a quote by

Abraham Lincoln, "Better to remain silent and be thought a fool than to speak out and remove all doubt."

Being an active listener also shows respect and lets the speaker know that you care about them. It also shows that for those few minutes, you put their needs above your own. This is an attribute I have struggled with in the past and now I work hard to improve my skill.

There's no better way to show how well you are listening, than asking for more information. This gives you a chance to look smart, interested and open to learning more/doing better. Most people are afraid of looking dumb and shy away from asking questions. Instead of looking dumb they remain dumb. Choose to get smarter about everything.

There is a fine line with finding answers on your own with research, asking some questions for clarification and asking too many questions, making you look inadequate for the task.

31. Adaptable

Are you able to handle change quickly? Can you jump into a situation when asked and make it better? Or do you complain because it is "not your problem"? Many times, a company will promote people who they know will "jump in with both feet" and make a difference.

32. Effective Communication Skills

Do you know how to properly communicate both in writing and verbally? Are your emails so long and filled with grammar mistakes that no one wants to read them? When you speak, do you use a lot of "ums", "ahs", "like" and other filler words that make you sound boring?

You may have lots of knowledge, but if you don't know how to properly communicate it, you will lose out on opportunities for advancement. Trust me, I have learned from this mistake. Now, I make certain that my communication, whether it is to a client or to executives within the company, is perfect.

33. Confident, Not Cocky

Being comfortable in your own skin and with not having to prove it to everyone else. That's confidence. Your actions will show your value without you ever having to tell anyone else. No one likes to be reminded that you were right; they will respect you more if you let them determine that for themselves. If you are too cocky, it will put people off, and they will not want to be around you. But there is a small amount of "cockiness" where you emit confidence, and you know you are right! People can feel it, just don't be too conceited.

34. Modest

Being modest is not a weakness. It is knowing your strengths and weaknesses and being strong enough emotionally to ask for help without feeling belittled. It is putting the good of the company above your need to look good. It's also about being humble. Let your great actions speak for themselves.

35. Team Player

Is everything about you, or about making your team and your company look good? Managers know who is doing their job and who is not. By trying to make others look good, you ultimately make yourself look good.

36. Help Your Boss Have a Great Work/Life Balance

Get that report done so he or she can leave a bit early for a kid's soccer game or school play. Ask if there is anything else you can do to help your boss get out on time.

37. Reward Upward

Remembering a boss' birthday or getting a cake to honor a promotion is not sucking up – it's a WOW. Most people don't think about the boss as a person. The things you might do for a co-worker or someone who reports to you are also great ways of showing your boss he or she is appreciated.

38. Make Sure They Know What's Going On

No boss wants an unwelcome surprise. If there is a problem, tell them first, the client or staff second. That goes for good news too. A boss who feels on top of things is a happy boss who looks like he or she is in charge.

There you have it, 38 ways to WOW and impress your boss. May you soon see the rewards of WOW in your work life! In the next chapter Raymond is going to explain how to WOW your clients to brand advocacy.

CHAPTER 6

How to WOW Your Clients to Brand Advocacy

Raymond's Insight

"People don't buy what you do, they buy why you do it."
—Simon Sinek

YOU ARE BRANDED whether you know not it or not and most likely badly! You may be wondering how could you be branded? Isn't that only for big companies and highly regarded geographical areas like Hawaii, New York, and Toronto? I have a secret to share with you. EVERYONE has a brand.

In my workshops, I often ask my participants to raise their hand if they know someone who always makes excuses for everything. Hands and sometimes jokingly legs are raised as a person's name pops into their head. Making excuses is actually that person's brand.

Let's say that person's name is Joe and he is a marketing director of a medium sized firm. If I talked to him and asked him if he has a brand, his first answer would be 'no' because he does not know what branding is. If I asked what impression he makes on his clients and customers, his answer would be positive descriptive words like 'knowledgeable,' 'good communications skills,' and 'produces excellent work.' Which just shows you how unaware most employees and entrepreneurs are of their own brand.

Now if I were to tell Joe that his brand was 'excuse maker,' he would deny it vehemently and be very upset that I even suggested that this is his brand, yet every one of his co-workers, bosses, and clients know it to be true. If you don't consciously grow your brand, it will be negative.

What is Branding?

There are two levels of branding, personal and business. When it comes to business, a brand is a proper name of a product that stands for something. It lives in the consumer's mind, has positive or negative characteristics, and invokes a feeling or an image. In short, it's a person's perception of a product or a company.

Branding is the science and art of making something that isn't unique, *unique*. Branding in the marketplace is the same as branding on a ranch. Ranchers use branding to differentiate their cattle from every other rancher's cattle. In the marketplace, branding is what makes a product stand out in a crowd of similar products. The right branding gets you noticed, remembered and bought.

Personal Branding

While corporate and product branding is important, what is more important is how branding applies to you personally. When you are branded properly it has these characteristics:

- ➤ Branding makes you trustworthy and known
- ➤ Branding differentiates you from others
- ➤ Branding makes you worth more money
- ➤ Branding pre-sells your product or service

So, what is good personal branding? Several things. First of all, it is visibility. Every single person who has high visibility makes a lot of money and has the ability to WOW more clients. Second is credibility or the promises that you make and the promises that you keep. Third, your brand is what others know about you. Fourth, it is how others perceive you, and lastly, when someone says WOW about you, you are well branded.

The Branding Ladder

Even if you do everything perfectly, branding takes time. How much time is hard to say, as some factors are beyond your control, but you can make it go faster by understanding the different levels and what is needed to reach each one.

Moving through the levels of branding is like climbing a ladder. The *Branding Ladder* has six specific rungs and unlike stairs, you can't take them two at a time, you have to take them in order. Also, some rungs you will spend more time on than others.

You can think of the Branding Ladder as a scale between -10 and +10, with an additional 2 bonus points for WOW. Everyone starts at zero or -10, if their brand is in trouble.

- Rung #1 Brand Distaste -10/12
    - Rung #2 Brand Indifference 0/12
        - Rung #3 Brand Awareness 1/12
            - Rung #4 Brand Preference 4/12
                - Rung #5 Brand Insistence 10/12
                    - Rung #6 Brand Advocacy 12/12

What does each one mean for you?

Rung #1 Brand Distaste

This is the place you do not want to be. Not only is the client aware of you but they are actively telling people NOT to do business with you. Why? Their experiences with you have been negative. You didn't keep the promises that you made to them. For example:

You are a writer and a professional speaker with a big following wants you to write their book. This is a huge step up for you and to impress them and get the job you make promises you can't keep. This client wants it done to coincide with a huge event they are doing, and you don't get it done in time. The client is upset and has to change things last minute.

Do you think that they are going to recommend you to their friends and other professionals they know? Of course not. They will tell them not to work with you.

This is a difficult place to be. Before you can even think of branding you need to improve your level of service so that clients you do get give you glowing reviews.

Rung #2 Brand Indifference (Living in a Void)

This is where 97% of people live. Nobody knows you and you don't have a brand. For you, life is tough. Sales are tough and you price cut to try to attract more clients. You work overtime, evenings and weekends and vacations are rare.

This level is way too common and is responsible for chronic overwork, failed marriages, ill-health and many other woes related to working way too hard for way too little money.

You are swimming around in the sea of sameness with every other realtor, (graphic designer, plumber, dentist), indistinguishable from every other person in your trade. There is nothing about you that rises above the rest and draws attention to yourself. The good news is that, unless you screw up, the only way to go is up. The only way to become different is to brand yourself.

The best way to brand yourself is to write your own book. This rises you above the sea of sameness. How does it do that? For example, one of my clients was a struggling car salesman. He came to me for help and I suggested that he write a book on the level of customer service you will receive when you buy a car from him and he lived up to that promise.

When talking to potential customers he would hand them the book. Think about it. What if you were that potential customer? You have already been to several dealerships and every sales person basically did the same thing and you left because you felt pressured to buy and then you walk into his dealership. Instead of feeling pressured you get handed a book and the salesman says to you, "My goal is to help you drive the car of your dreams and I have it in writing, to prove it."

Do you think that salesman is going to stand out in your mind especially once you start reading the book and see what he is going to do for you? Yes, he will and that is what happens. Now he has a huge base of customers who will ONLY deal with him.

If you are interested in writing your book but don't know where to start check out my (Raymond's) 10-10-10 Program™ at www.10-10-10program.com where I will guide you step by step to having you book finished and physical copies in your hand in 10 weeks.

Rung #3 Brand Awareness

This is the first upward motion you have on the Branding Ladder. It is a very good place to be because most people and businesses never get there.

Awareness is nice – it's better to be at least known versus unknown. But, don't take too much comfort at this level. Simply paying for a huge billboard in the middle of town will ensure that you are known by many, many more thousands of people. But, awareness alone does not well translate into sales. You may know of Rolls Royce, but it does not do the Rolls Royce salesman any good if you are never going to buy one. You want people to be aware of you.

How do you increase awareness to the point that they want to work with you? By providing value and then WOWing them with it and yes, one of the ways to do that is with your book.

Your book opens doors to not only being seen in the marketplace but valued which leads to . . .

Rung #4 Brand Preference

When you reach this rung, you will start to see some results from your branding. Your clients see a real difference between you and your competition, and you are their first choice.

You are a bit better than others. You call back faster; you get your work done quicker or you might have a slightly better price. These are good reasons for your client to choose you over others, but they may not be good enough all the time.

If your level of service drops in any way, you will quickly lose your brand preference. At this level, it is about scalability. You need to be focusing on the business of the business, not the content of the business. What do I mean by that? You need to be working on your business, not inside of your business. There hits a time when you need to bring other people to do the things that you are not good at, so you can focus your time and energy on the things that make your business money.

If you try to do everything yourself eventually your clients will suffer and go to someone else.

Rung #5 Brand Insistence

When your clients want ONLY your products and services and won't accept a substitute then you will have reached the fifth rung. This is a coveted place to be because it means that you have risen above all others and your clients are loyal to the point where they won't go anywhere else.

It means that your attrition (that means loss of existing clients) will be low to zero. It means that you do not have to spend marketing money or time to get new business from those who are already insistent on using you. You put something out there and they buy it from you and no one else.

Apple is a perfect example of brand insistence. When the company introduces a new product, many of its brand insistent fans will wait in line overnight to be one of the first to have it. In their eyes, no one is better than the late, Steve Jobs!

For me it's Starbucks. If I want coffee and there is no Starbucks, I will not buy coffee. Period.

Rung #6 Brand Advocacy

Brand Advocacy is better than 10 out of 10 because your clients are so happy with you, your service or your product that they tell everyone to use it. They are your uber-fans who tell everyone including strangers how wonderful you are. Most people can only dream of this level of loyalty and promotion. People who are your Brand Advocates do these five activities:

- ✓ Enthusiastically and continually give you word-of-mouth referrals.
- ✓ Advertise you and your business for free.
- ✓ Tell others how credible you are.
- ✓ Pre-sell prospective clients on your products and services.
- ✓ Increase your profits by becoming money-making machines that increase sales and decrease marketing costs.

How to WOW Your Customers Up The Branding Ladder

You only have less than a second to make a first impression and start moving your potential clients up the *branding ladder*. I already talked about one of the main ways and that is to have your own book but there are others and let's focus in on three of them.

Business Card

What is the purpose of your business card? Your business card is not an information document. Its main purpose is to be a marketing machine because most of the people that you are giving it to are potential prospects. They don't need information like your address; it is not necessary at this point to get the sale.

Designing Your Business Card

1. What should you be selling with your business card? It is not your product or service. It should be something

that brings value to the prospect and encourages them to take action. You can give away a special report such as *7 Ways To Get Rid Of Back Pain* or *The 4 Worst Things A Company Does When Buying Office Supplies*. You can also have people call for a free consultation.

2. What to put on the card? Your name. An impressive title like 'Award Winning Author,' that relates to what you want people to do. Then a call to action such as, "Call my private phone number for a free consultation," and then your phone number or website. Include your picture only if you know that it will increase the odds of someone taking action.

3. Have the right email address. Email addresses have a brand. Hotmail has the lowest brand email address there is. Rich, successful people who see that will not want to work with you and you will not know why.

4. Make your design stand out. Change your card so that it looks different from everyone else's card. Make the shape or colour different. For example, if you are realtor make it the shape of a house. Yes, it will cost more, but it will be worth it when you get the client over someone else.

Communication Skills

The junior purpose of communication is a transfer of data. The senior purpose of communication is intimacy. If you want to create an instant connection, then you need to raise the level of your communication. The higher or more successful a person is, the better your skills need to be.

What are some of the common mistakes that people make?

1. Using verbal fossils such as 'um,' 'ah,' and 'like.' They make you sound unprofessional and like you don't know what you are talking about.
2. Use of small talk. Common people use small talk. Successful people have meaningful conversations.
3. Use of weak verbs, such as try, hope, and want.
4. Giving a Preamble. It is the explanation and back story you give before you ask a question. The preamble is never interesting, except to the speaker.

Keep Your Promises

Excuses will kill your brand faster than office gossip. When you are given an opportunity to WOW someone, don't mess it up with low quality work and then excuses as to why you couldn't even deliver that.

The best way to move your new client up the branding ladder fast is to produce high-quality work that you deliver before it is due and then do that something extra that creates loyalty right from the start.

5 Simple Ways to WOW Your Clients

1. Personalize communications and products or services. Dell Computers lost their brand but, when the company was new, they were successful because users built their own computers by being able to opt

for more memory or including an internal CD/DVD drive. MacDonald's used to let you have it your way and Build-a-Bear let's kids design the stuffed animal of their dreams.

2. Deliver products in an unexpected way. Amazon is using drones and actual, physical stores for more immediate gratification. Don't use FedEx if a messenger can get there faster. Better still, if you're in the neighborhood, hand deliver the package to your customer.

3. Include free updates and accessories. This works especially well for software companies but is highly adaptable to other types of business. Consultants can revisit the numbers six months later, stores or websites can enhance the product use experience by including a carrying case or stylus with a tablet or computer. No, I'm not suggesting your give away the next generation of a product, but you can offer current customers a higher trade-in discount or an early-bird purchase date.

Conversely, continue to service older product models or generations of software. Give lifetime guarantees or, at the very least, remove all restrictions. Can you imagine how people would feel if Samsung phone insurance covered dropping your phone into water or cracked screens?

4. Include a hand-written note. No one writes out personalized messages. They sometimes pretend to, but customers can always tell that something has been printed out by computer. This is a great way to

show how special you think your customer is. Large companies can't do it – too expensive, but you can.

5. Make customer service and satisfaction a priority. Free delivery used to be a WOW, but now is a given because everyone started doing it. Reach out to your customers and ask if they are happy with their purchase or service, send reminder emails, eliminate all restrictions on returns, have knowledgeable service agents who are empowered to fix customer problems themselves.

It's Time to Start

Here is the biggest benefit to branding, it allows your business to work harder for you than you work for it. Branding allows you to earn more in a month than you earned all last year. Branding allows me to take a one-week vacation each month and a one-month vacation every year, and such blessings are available for you too.

Now in the next chapter Ash is going to share with you How To Create A Team of WOW With Your Staff/Co-Workers. When you are well branded and you work with a team that knows how to create WOW, there is nothing that will stop you.

CHAPTER 7

How to Create a Team of WOW With Your Staff/Co-Workers

Ash's Wisdom

"Great things are done by a series of small things that are brought together."

—Vincent Van Gogh

THERE CAME A defining moment on my WOW journey. When I was in the printing industry, I did work for an important company. I spent time with the CEO and managers, created all types of marketing materials and gave them good advice. They always felt like they were my only customer and they were shocked when they found out that they weren't. I had always made them feel like they were the only one without even realizing what I had done.

One day they came to me and said they didn't have a structured customer service department. They had people calling the warehouse to solve their problems. The CEO said to me, "You are a printer, and a graphic designer, but I want to hire you as a consultant for WOW. I need you to go in and create structure and help our customers."

I had no experience with that particular industry and of course, I am a salesman, not a customer service manager but I never back down from a challenge. They threw me in the water and said, 'sink or swim,' and I had to train myself.

They sent me every customer case they had. Most customer service issues were six-eight weeks old, with no resolution in sight. I was able to turn that around and create a structured customer service department. Response time went down to two or three days. I found the problem and resolved it by making quick decisions and then taking the appropriate action quickly.

Eventually, customer service was taken over by somebody else. We trained her, and I helped to create a customer service manual so the level of service would stay the same. Now, I didn't do this all on my own. I came up with ideas and oversaw the project but it was the people I was working with that really made the transformation possible and that it what this chapter is about. Any business that wants to be successful has to have a WOW staff who see the vision of the company and are willing to work together to see it come to fruition.

How to Create A WOW Team

Creating a WOW team, for me, begins with the hiring process. I want to find the right people BEFORE I hire them. I want to know that they have the basics required for them to fit in well, with my WOW team. So, what sort of things do I look for? I think that you are going to be surprised.

Creativity

One thing I look for always during the interview process is creativity and, no, I don't mean just artists. For me creativity means the ability to create from nothing. They can come to a situation and start from scratch. Is that person able to be creative?

Can he or she come in and not focus on the problem but the solution? If all they do is come to me and say, "That is not possible, I can't do this or that can't be done." They are not the right person for the job. It is the opposite of what I need. They don't need to always have an answer but they have to be able to search for one.

Enthusiasm

Enthusiasm is the ability or willingness to do things outside of the what is expected in a normal hiring process, like tell me a joke, sing me a song or, here is a small object, take it apart and put it back together again. Things you wouldn't expect. Their ability to handle unexpected situations will show a lot about how they will deal with problems and other people on the team. If they are willing to try to do what I ask, even if it is unconventional, that show's they are a team player.

Willing to Consider Someone Else's Viewpoint

I ask potential employees when was the last time you changed your mind about something or someone? I want to know whether this person must always be right or if they will listen to another's viewpoint, carefully consider what what's being said, and then determine the best course of action, even if it is not their idea in the first place.

It doesn't have to be ground shaking either. Someone can say to me, "I have always hated peas, but last week I was on a date and I was embarrassed to say that I hate peas. So, I tried them and you know what? I loved them."

Proper Balance

Another question I ask is, "What do you love to do in your spare time - for you?" For example, something active or artsy. Something you do to be creative or for mental/emotional release. So, if I ask the question and he says, "Oh I love to skateboard." "Great when was the last time you skateboarded?" "Well 15 years ago." Well, then you are not really committed to having balance in your life.

It is important in life to have ways of dealing with stress and someone who only works with no outlets in life will burn-out or their body will give out leaving the company stranded and rushing to try to find someone who can step in.

Resilience

For me that is mental toughness. So, I would ask them things like, "What is the toughest situation you have ever been in?" When they tell me a situation where they have been overwrought, and how they worked themselves out of it, then I know that they have coping skills.

How to Create a Team of WOW With Your Staff/Co-Workers

One area I focus in on is their email inbox. How does a person deal with 500 things in their inbox? Do they tackle them and get them taken care of or do they do a few here and a few there so, maybe, the other person gets a response in two to three days?

To have a WOW team, my people need to be able to co-cycle. Go through their emails, make a decision and take action. If they don't have the ability to make a decision, then they are of no help to me. It doesn't mean that a person goes rogue and does whatever they want but they have to be able to make decisions quickly in the context of their job. They also have to have a good sense of when they need my approval and when they can act on their own say so.

Taking Responsibility

I want to know if this person I am looking to hire will take responsibility for their life or blames others for what has happened to them. So, I ask them, "Why did you leave your last job?" If they spend the next 15 minutes blaming their managers, their executives, their co-workers and the people that work under them, then I am not going to hire them.

Think on Their Feet

Part way through the interview I will quickly ask an ad-lib question to see if they can think quickly. Something along the lines of, "How do they handle an irate customer, employee, or colleague? What would they do?" If they can give me a quick answer that makes sense then that is what I am looking for. If they can't answer something simple like that, then they are not good material for my WOW team.

Professional Appearance

Part of WOW is the pride that you take in your appearance. If you come to meet me for the first time, and your shirt is untucked and your hair is oily and greasy and you are 15 minutes late, there is a good chance you are going to be that way the whole time you are working. I want people who have a WOW presence, not someone that shows up and comes in and annoys people.

Technology

I want someone who is willing to change and adapt to technology, no matter what age, even if they have to go back to school. So, I give them a test to see how wise they are with technology. I ask them to have a meeting on Skype. If they tell me that they have never been on Skype, I ask them to get on it. I want to see how fast are they willing to adapt. If they aren't willing to learn then they are not who I am looking for.

The Vindictive Blame Game

I have had people come in and tell me, "At my last job, I screwed my boss over and I was happy to see him fail. I warned him that his decision was going to come back to haunt him, and he had to eat crow and I made sure he did." First off, that's unacceptable. Worse, they don't know it's unacceptable and actually told me the truth.

As soon as I hear that, I know that person will do the same thing to me and his colleagues. They don't care about the company only themselves. Vindictiveness only causes unWOW in any company.

Adaptable

Can they switch gears, learn a new software program or work in a different way? How easily can they change their tone or style to make a customer feel more comfortable?

I ask them a question that they have to find the answer for. Are they willing to first admit they don't know something and second are they willing to go look for the answer? If they are then I know that they will adapt. If they fight me on it, they are not a good fit. I will watch them research and ask questions on the topic that I need answers for. This is usually reserved for a second interview and not on the first.

Questions

Another thing I do is look at the kind of questions I get asked. I always look for good, innovative, and fun questions. If one of the first questions is, "What does the job pay?" then I already know that all they are interested in is the money and not the company and I probably won't hire them.

What are some of the great questions asked? "What is the best thing about working here?" or "What is the culture of the company?" I look for the best questions they ask me about the company itself. Their inquisitiveness about who they are working for, not just the standard ones about pay and hours.

How to Keep The WOW Going With Your Existing Staff/Co-workers?

To continue to create WOW, you need to continue to do things together, you take part in social things. You remember each other's birthdays, you remember to congratulate.

Acknowledge the wins, make sure everybody knows when a sales person makes a goal. Let the company share it, so the team can email each other, and tell them that they did a great job.

You take courses and classes together. When we have a course, we try to get as many people at the course as we can. Have an atmosphere of positive communication and everyone knows the policies surrounding that. Continue to grow and learn together. Are they a willing participant or full of excuses not to be able to attend?

Let people know that they matter and that the contributions they make are important to the company. Keep these things going continually and you will see results.

What Are The Results of a WOW Team

For me it looks like three things. First a well-oiled machine that works together with no problems. Second and this is my favourite analogy and that is a thousand, cohesive, artful and magically moving ants. They all move in the same direction at the same time and you always wonder how they do it. The third is basketball. Executing plays skillfully, people are moving and dribbling back and forth, and their teammates know where they are going to be because they know the playbook like the back of their hand. That is what a WOW team looks like.

In chapter 8 Raymond is going to cover something unusual that will set your company apart from all others and make it successful. This is how you take customer service to the next level and I know you are going to enjoy it!

CHAPTER 8

The Directors of WOW and unWOW

Raymond's Wisdom

"An exceptional company is the one that gets all the little details right. And the people out on the front line, they know when things are not going right, and they know when things need to be improved. And if you listen to them, you can soon improve all those niggly things which turn an average company into an exceptional company."

—Sir Richard Branson

KATELYN SAT IN the crowded airport with all her luggage and Justin, a squirming three-year-old who was tired, hungry, and all around miserable. To be honest, she didn't feel much better. She was flying across the country to say goodbye to her dying father. The doctors said he had less than a day left, and she prayed that she could get there in time.

But the plane was already three hours late and Katelyn just wanted to scream at someone, but she didn't. Finally, an hour later the plane arrived, by that time Katelyn was on her last nerve.

As she went up to the flight attendant with her boarding passes, she was told to wait to the side. "What now?" Katelyn thought to herself. Can't she just get on the plane and try to get her son asleep so could have a few minutes of peace and quiet before dealing with the hardest day of her life?

"I'm sorry Miss Piper but the plane is sold out, and you will have to wait for the next one." "What do you mean sold out? I have my tickets that I paid an arm and a leg for right here." "Well, Miss Piper we always oversell tickets because on 99% of flights people don't show up. This time everyone did, and you were the last one to buy a ticket." "You don't understand, my Dad is dying, and this is my last chance to see him. If I don't get on that flight, he could be gone by the time I get there. Please, I will do anything, just get me on that flight!" "I am sorry to hear that Miss but there is nothing that I can do about that. If you want to go back to the ticket counter, they can see about getting you on another flight." With that, the flight attendant went through the gangway doors and closed them leaving Katelyn high and dry.

Katelyn stood there for a moment stunned. How could they do this to her? She told the person when she booked the tickets the details, and they said that she would be on this flight. She rushed to the ticket counter, hoping against all hope that there was another flight soon but there wasn't. When Katelyn burst into tears, the gentleman coldly told her that she would have to move away from the counter as he had other customers to serve.

The Directors of WOW and unWOW

Half an hour later she received the call that her father had passed away. Katelyn vowed that not only would she never fly with that company again, but she would make sure that everyone knew why and as a reporter for a big city newspaper that wasn't going to be hard . . .

Almost everyone has a horror story about how they were mistreated in a store, kept on hold for an hour or treated like cattle at the airport. In these days of low-grade customer experiences, even the smallest WOW can make your business grow like gangbusters, and that is where your Director of WOW and unWOW comes in.

If you own a company, then you need a Director of WOW. Don't confuse a marketing director or a regular customer service representative with a Director of WOW. If you ARE the company, then make time to plan your WOW actions. WOWing your customers and having your employees onboard, needs to be a priority in your business if you want it to grow and succeed.

The Director of WOW

This is the person who is in charge of creating a culture in your business where WOW can thrive. These Directors think outside of the box of what customer service is, in fact, they don't even consider it customer service, it is how the business is run. The goal is to create surprise and delight in the customers. The easy way is to remember the word BUMPER.

Big: The bigger the WOW, the more your client is going to be amazed.

Unexpected: Make your WOWs a surprise to the customer

Memorable: Make your WOWs memorable. Things that are remembered get talked about.

Positive: Make the WOW experience so positive that it makes an impact.

Extra: Make you WOW above and beyond the normal confines of the product or service.

Relevant: Make the WOW relevant to the product or service.

Create a Culture of WOW

So how do you create that culture within your team, so that they will promote and execute WOW every day? It starts with your vision. You have to know what WOW looks like for your company, don't expect your employees to do it. It must start from the top down.

Second, is the ability to communicate that vision. It must be imparted in such a way that it becomes alive to your team of employees.

Third, is creating specific WOW actions. Put a system of WOW in place that includes all the elements of BUMPER for each position.

Fourth is to create accountability and encourage each employee to take responsibility for what they can do. Have daily or weekly meetings where you cover what WOWs happened. Let people share ideas on what is working and what is not.

Fifth is to equip them. Provide financial means for them to easily WOW customers. Set budgets on what they can spend and then train them in how to use the money.

Sixth is reward them. When you hear reports of customers and clients being WOWed then reward the staff who provided it. Make it fun for the employees to provide WOW.

The Director of unWOW

The main focus of the Director of unWOW is to create WOWs from bad situations that occur. Sometimes it can be employees, or it can just be things out of the company's control. No matter what it is, the Director not only needs to make it right but bring it to a WOW situation.

Let me share an example from Carol's life. It was Christmas Eve 2015 and Carol was so looking forward to spending Christmas Day with her family eating good food that she had cooked.

She had gone out a few days earlier and had bought some new deep-dish pie plates to make the family's favourite apple and pumpkin pies and was now making them on Christmas Eve. Everything was perfect, the apple pie was done and cooling on the stove, and the two pumpkin pies were in the stove and ready to come out.

As she lifted the first one out, **BOOM!!!** The pie plate exploded as it touched the top of the stove and sent glass everywhere. Thankfully, Carol was able to jump back as it happened and no glass cut her, but it had gone everywhere including the apple pie on top of the stove and the pumpkin pie in the stove. All the desserts were ruined.

After the shock wore off and her husband had cleaned up the glass, she was so upset, all of the desserts for Christmas Day destroyed. She just sat and cried while her daughter and husband tried to console her. She did manage from the few ingredients she had in the house to pull together a small dessert that barely fed everyone, but it almost ruined Carol's Christmas and she was going to do something about it . . .

On December 27th, she called the customer service line for the company who had made the plates. She expected some grumpy person, who would question her honesty, hassle her and maybe send her one plate, but she was completely surprised by what happened next.

The gentleman who answered the phone was polite, even friendly. He listened to her whole story without interruption. When he heard what occurred the first words out of his mouth were, "Are you ok? Was anyone hurt? I am so sorry that this happened and ruined your Christmas."

He then went on to tell her, that not only would he replace all the glass pie plates she had bought with the highest quality ceramic ones, but he also gave her $75 credit to buy whatever she wanted from their online cooking/baking supply store. He also promised that once she sent him the list, he would have the products to her within a few days.

Carol was shocked and thanked the man. She went onto the website and got herself some things that she had wanted for a while, but just didn't have the money to buy and emailed him the list. She got discouraged when she hadn't heard back from him and was going to call in just after the New Year to give him what for, but before she could there was a knock on her door one day, and there stood a delivery guy with a big box just for her.

When she opened it, there was everything the customer service man had promised. I guess with it being the Christmas Season, he hadn't had a chance to email her, but he made sure that the products came quickly. It was like Christmas morning all over again. Even now after all this time, she still uses the gifts that she got and tells people about the wonderful service she received.

That is what the Director of unWOW does, takes a negative experience that could bring a brand down and changes them into Brand Ambassadors.

I encourage you to take the time to focus on creating WOW experiences for your customers and clients. When you put them first, you will find that your business skyrockets and you will never lack for customers because your brand will be so high.

CHAPTER 9

Springing Into Action

Ash's Final Words

"There are risks and costs to action. But they are far less than the long-range risks of comfortable inaction."
—John F. Kennedy

IN THE MOVIE Braveheart, William Wallace WOWed a nation because he chose to act. He had decided that the status quo was not good enough for him or his people any longer and did something about it. His continual actions sparked a whole group of people to change their fate and their lives forever.

Action is what changes unWOWs and even average, mediocre things into WOWs that make a difference. So, why is it important to start taking action now?

Now is the only time you have. The past is gone and the future is uncertain. When you procrastinate you delay your destiny for one more day, one more month, one more year or even one more decade. It is one of worst things that you can possibly do.

You don't have to do anything as dramatic as starting a revolution, but you do have to do something or you are not going to see any change. Start with small decisions, followed by incremental steps. Progress is always about the small decisions because, when taken together, they make for great changes.

Make a decision, any decision doesn't matter if it is right or wrong because making it will empower you to keep moving forward. So many people are afraid of making decisions that they eventually stall and get left behind by everyone else. That's not the worst of it, staying still often ends up by moving backwards. So, any decision is better than no decision.

If you are not sure about a certain subject, don't know what to do on a website or can't figure out what reward to give your employee, just make a quick decision. I have seen people who cannot make decisions and the profound affect it has on their lives. They struggle even when driving a car, whether to turn right or left, take the highway, not take the highway, this street, that street; they are so self-conscious about being wrong, or making the wrong decision or even experiencing failure that they don't move forward.

Make the first change now, and stop being indecisive. Even the smallest decision will help you to move forward. Waiting is just going to cause more un-Wow's in your life, and keep you in a dream/wish state. It's okay to have hopes and dreams, but it is not okay if that is all you do, right? Sometimes, it's better to make a decision, go forward and fail. The most successful people are those who have failed the most. Think of Thomas Edison and Albert Einstein.

Also, if you want to move forward and create a life of WOW, you need to stop looking or living in the past. That is just a waste of time and energy, focusing on something that you can't change. The same people who won't make decisions for their future are also the ones stuck in the past. They don't see that circumstances change and different people show up in their lives. So, they assume what didn't work in the past will never work. Some of the best ideas get killed this way.

Always making decisions based assuming that you will get the same results as you did ten/fifteen/twenty years ago is is a form of lunacy. You will be wrong! I have seen normally rational people turn down good business because they are afraid of losing money just as they lost it fifteen years ago.

They don't want to make a decision because they are afraid they are going to lose a partner yet again. They don't pick a partner because they are afraid he or she is going to suffocate them like their first associate did. So, they never move forward. Everything about them is based in the past. It becomes a problem.

Making decisions this way is a ticket to hell because you are going to be stuck in a very small place, in a very small job, in a very small life, in a very small relationship or in no relationship at all. These people are always afraid that others are out to get them. They have either a conspiracy mentality or the *I am always right, everybody is always wrong, no one wants to see me succeed but me* attitude. They have such an ill-will feeling about human nature, and it is not the truth. I see it all of the time.

The Starting Place For Personal WOW

It starts with making those incremental decisions we talked about earlier. Change your attitude, change the way you look, change your surroundings, buy a painting, say yes to that date that you initially refused, or get online and take a course. It's about totally changing your comfort zone so you can become the best YOU that creates the best WOWS. Just ask a woman with a new hairstyle or her first power dress. Or your cousin who just bought her first house. They immediately become more of who they want to be.

Let's say that you hate bagels. Why don't you try something different? Get a bagel from another store, try a different flavour. You hate milk, and have since you were five-years-old. Have you tried drinking it since you were five-years-old? Things have changed in your life since then. Is it possible your taste buds have changed too? That's not uncommon. Becoming a WOW person means opening yourself up to new experiences and growing as a person.

> *"In order to do something, you've never done, you've got to become someone you've never been."*
> —Les Brown

I love this quote, and it is true but I believe that the reverse is true as well. To become someone you have never been, you have to do things you have never done. If your goal is to become the best spouse in the world who WOWs your husband or wife all the time, then guess what? You will have to change. I can guarantee it. Unless you and your spouse have the exact same personality types, love languages and share all the same interests, you will have to work on something to WOW your spouse. Start by seeing things from their point-of-view. Favorite color? Hidden pleasure? Something they talk about but never get to try?

The same goes for all your relationships. To have WOW family and friends, you need to become a person who can adjust to many different situations. I am not saying that you have to change who you are in your core but you may want to express it differently.

For example, you have a friend and there is conflict between you because you disagree on politics very strongly. It is getting to the point where the conflict is affecting the relationship. So, how do you inject WOW into the situation? Do you have to change your views to keep the friendship? No, but you can choose not to talk about it and focus on things that you do agree on. If the other person brings it up, you can choose to just listen and not argue about it. Just because you disagree on something doesn't mean you have to be vocal about it.

Can you try to see it from their side? Can you find one thing you agree on? Then agreement can at least start without giving up what you believe or who you are.

When you work on yourself and make the important relationships in your life a priority, you will start to see WOW in ways you never expected. Sometimes creating WOWs can mean removing certain people from your life if the relationship with them is not moving you forward.

You don't need to cut everyone not perfectly aligned with you, but you do want to really look at those who are putting unWOWs in your path. Everyone needs to lean on a friend at some point but there are people who always lean and never provide a shoulder. If you let them exhaust you, you will not have the energy you need for yourself and everyone else in your life. Neighbor always complaining, cousin constantly criticizing you, even in jest? Avoid them as often as you can.

The Starting Place For Professional WOW

There are three things I recommend if you want to create WOW professionally. The first has to do with having affinity in your relationships in the work place. The person that you have always had a problem with, is there a way to improve the situation? Maybe. When you find something to connect the two of you, the relationship will change.

Start by finding out more about them and their personal life, trying to make a connection. There was once a co-worker I was having problems with, and I wanted to change that, so I asked him about his family and we connected based on our both having kids. Eventually that led to his total love for his grandkids, that was it. That became a catalyst for change, and a starting place for us to improve things. Heck, even talking about the bad relationships from our past in a comical way helped us to create a connection, and we could laugh about things after that. Laughter was not even on the table for this person and I before I added WOW to the situation. If you look, almost everyone has something you can use to connect with them, like pets, summer trips, or an elderly parent who needs your help. Just look and listen.

Springing Into Action

Second, if you really hate your job, you are not doing anyone, including you and your family, a favor by staying there. If you are miserable at work, you are miserable at home, and you are miserable to yourself. So, you might as well make a change. But, that doesn't mean quitting tomorrow. You may need to make small changes before you make the bigger ones, taking night courses (like I did), joining network groups, etc. With a bit of patience, it will payoff in the end.

Third, give yourself growth opportunities. Show your boss that you can do more. Shadow someone who has a skill that you want to learn and take on the responsibility of the job you want before you actually ask for it, if possible. Do it without it affecting your current job, and do it without extra pay. WOW your boss by being generous with your time.

Let me share a story with you from my life so you can see how it works. I used to be employed by a large, well-known department store. I started with them when I was just 16-years-old and it took decisive actions to get there. I had tried to get a job at this department store for a year straight and they kept saying 'no,' and I didn't know why. They had a fashion program for students that was called the Fashion Counsel. It was made up of teenagers, and my best friend got accepted and I didn't.

I remember going in there, and I remember looking at the manager of the entire area, and I said, "This is where I want to work. I am willing to learn, I am willing to do whatever it takes to get on the Fashion Counsel." I went further, and took in fashion drawings I had done for a course at school. That small WOW sealed it. I must have made an impression because I got the job the next week and was on the Counsel the following year. It was the greatest success of my life up to that point.

I made it a priority to make that job my own and to learn everything I could in that department. When I had been there nine months, I started learning about other areas of the job and I noticed that the sales people got commission and that they got paid a lot more than me.

I was 17-years-old at this point and wet behind the ears. I remember talking to my manager and saying, "I want to go work in shoes. I want to be a commission sales person," and she said, "Oh that is not possible. That doesn't work for me." I love challenges, so for me the game was on, and I was going to win. I waited, and as soon as a position opened up in that department, I took it even though there was no increase in pay.

The minute I got there, I turned into one of the top sales people, and the commission was amazing, it literally doubled or tripled my income. So, while people were making $10/$12/$15 an hour, I was making approximately $25 to $30 at that time. I was 17! It was so empowering.

The lesson is don't depend on other people to create YOUR WOW; create your own. Sometimes it means you may have to sacrifice, you may not get the money you want right away, and you may not get the prestige you want right away, but you will build to it, you will get there. I found that in every job I did.

So, again, take incremental steps towards WOW on the job, create WOW for your surroundings, WOW your co-workers. Do this with sincerity and with affinity.

Springing Into Action

We're Finally Here

It's hard to believe that this is the end of the book. When you write, you work hard to get to this point, but, now that it is here I am not sure that I want it to end. Creating WOW has changed my life and I want it to change yours too, so maybe this isn't the end.

Why don't you come over to www.awcreativemedia.com and check out what I can do for you? You can also check my artistic pieces at www.ashwalani.com If you need any of these things below, then let's continue the conversation relationship and let me show you WOW in person.

- Graphic Design
- Sales Team Management
- Art Direction
- Campaign Management
- Email Marketing
- Customer Service Management

From my heart to yours, I send you this blessing. May your life be filled with love, joy, happiness, fulfillment and most of all Wondrous Outstanding Worth.

www.ingramcontent.com/pod-product-compliance
Lightning Source LLC
Chambersburg PA
CBHW050649160426
43194CB00010B/1868